Complimentary Re...

EDWARD ELGAR:
MEMORIES OF A VARIATION

OXFORD UNIVERSITY PRESS
AMEN HOUSE, E.C. 4
London Edinburgh Glasgow New York
Toronto Melbourne Capetown Bombay
Calcutta Madras
HUMPHREY MILFORD
PUBLISHER TO THE UNIVERSITY

EDWARD AND ALICE ELGAR
At Garmisch, Bavarian Highlands. About 1894

EDWARD ELGAR:

MEMORIES OF A VARIATION

BY

MRS. RICHARD POWELL

OXFORD UNIVERSITY PRESS
LONDON NEW YORK TORONTO
1937

17492 [83]

To the Memory
of
A. J. J.

FOREWORD

I<small>N</small> writing a book such as this, which depends upon
diaries, letters, and memories, one finds that it falls
naturally into chronological sequence.

The principal difficulty has been to avoid turning it into
something uncomfortably like an autobiography. To make
the bits and scraps of which it is composed to some extent
continuous, and to explain things in general, it has been
necessary for me to appear more than I should wish.

My thanks are due to Mrs. Elgar Blake and to Mrs.
Hunter, as well as to the executors of the late Sir Edward
Elgar, for permission to reprint letters to me from Sir
Edward Elgar and Mr. A. J. Jaeger respectively; to
Messrs. Reginald Haines, Histed, and Window and
Groves for permission to use portraits by them; and to
Miss May Grafton for permission to reproduce the photo-
graph of Sir Edward taken in the study at Plâs Gwyn.

D. M. P.

APRIL, 1937

PREFACE

Woodend, Broadheath
near Worcester
Dec. 5th, 1936

MY DEAR DORA

You have given me the very pleasant task of bestowing my blessing on your reminiscences of what were, in spite of the difficulties and worries attendant on the life of a genius and the making of a career, such happy days. And I do it most willingly because I am grateful to you for this faithful and vivid picture of my parents. There is no such record except in the memories of those who were associated with them. You have also shown so beautifully the wonderful unselfishness and devotion of my Mother and the inspiration and help of 'Nimrod'.

I have been reduced to a condition of helplessness over the scenes you describe, of which I recall so many. Those who know anything of our home life will live them again with mingled tears and laughter—to those who do not it will come perhaps as a revelation that the home life of a genius could be so happy and spontaneous, and contain none of the freakish elements which for some unexplained reason are inevitably associated with it.

Yours affectionately

CARICE ELGAR BLAKE.

CONTENTS

LIST OF ILLUSTRATIONS

1895

I FIRST met Edward Elgar on December 6th, 1895. He and Mrs. Elgar came to Wolverhampton at the invitation of my step-mother. They came to luncheon, spent the afternoon, and had tea. My father had been made Rector of Wolverhampton in the spring of that year and in the following August he married Miss Mary Frances Baker, of Hasfield, near Gloucester. With Miss Baker came a very substantial addition in the furniture line to our large Rectory, and the connexion with her brought us a host of most delightful new friends.

Caroline Alice Roberts, daughter of General Sir Henry Gee Roberts, K.C.B., was one of a group of girl friends who studied geology with the Rev. William Samuel Symonds, Rector of Pendock, Worcestershire. They used to go fossil-hunting on the banks of the Severn, and my mother tells of the delightful times they had and what an interesting and dear friend Mr. Symonds was to all of them. They called him 'the Professor'. Later on Alice Roberts, who lived with her mother at Redmarley, took accompaniment lessons from a Mr. Elgar who was teacher of the violin at Worcester High School when Miss Ottley was headmistress.

'Dear Alice!' my mother says, 'How hard she worked at it. She nearly wore her fingers to the bone practising and I couldn't think what for. She would never have made a fine player.'

After the death of Lady Roberts Alice went abroad for a time and then settled down at a little house in

Malvern Link called Ripple Lodge. There she went on with her accompaniment lessons, and before long the mystery was solved—she and Mr. Elgar became engaged to be married. They came over to see Miss Baker at Hasfield and he was terribly shy and quiet! They were married in 1889 and went to live in London, in Marloes Road. Miss Baker stayed with them there. Two years after the birth of their daughter, Carice (now Mrs. Elgar Blake), they stayed with Miss Baker at Hasfield. It was summer time and very hot. He used to bring in hedgehogs from the woods and feed them in the house. He sat in the strawberry bed and wished that some one would bring him champagne in a bedroom jug. As he was deep in ideas for *The Black Knight* this is not surprising.[1]

In 1892 Miss Baker took them to Bayreuth. They heard *Parsifal, Tannhäuser, Die Meistersinger*; and *Parsifal* for a second time the night before they left. This was his first experience of Wagner, and who can say what a wonderful revelation it must have been to him. He was wild with enthusiasm and delight. From Bayreuth they went to Heidelberg and then on into the Bavarian Highlands.

I once got him on to the subject of that Bayreuth Festival—years later, sitting on a bank looking at the Severn.

> She did give us a splendid time—I called her 'the Mascotte' —did you know that? I made her stamp and post the manuscript of *The Black Knight* when it went off to Novello's. We posted it at Heidelberg. I said she would bring me luck and so she did.

[1] E. E. always spoke of the theme at Scene 4, Letter G, as the 'Perrier Jouet' theme.

2

I seem to have digressed somewhat, but picture us now, my mother and me, tramming up to the station at Wolverhampton to meet them, on Friday, December 6th, 1895. The train came in and, of course, not having seen one another for an age, the two friends fell upon each other and Mr. Elgar was left for me to look after. I quickly found out that music was the last thing he wanted to talk about. I think we talked about football. He wanted to know if I ever saw the Wolverhampton Wanderers play, and when he heard that our house was a stone's throw from their ground he was quite excited.

'Can't we go and see a match to-day?'

'There isn't one, I'm afraid; it's a Friday.'

'I shall come again on a Saturday. Will you take me to a match?'

He came into the drawing-room before luncheon: 'Hullo, there's the black piano! Let's see how its inside has stood the move.'

Although I had not left school very long I had heard a number of good pianists, but I had never heard anything quite like this. He didn't play like a pianist, he almost seemed to play like a whole orchestra. It sounded full without being loud and he contrived to make you hear other instruments joining in. It fascinated me then and always. But how difficult it was to turn over for him! When it came to playing from his own manuscripts you often saw nothing but a few pencilled notes and a mark or two, when he was playing something tremendous—full orchestra and chorus perhaps.

'Well, why don't you turn over?'

In time I think I became rather clever at it, and loved

3

nothing better. When I came to know them very well it was the usual thing, almost directly after I arrived, for me to slide into a seat by the piano ready to turn over with just the greeting, 'There you are. That's all right.'

But to return.

After luncheon that first day we all went to the drawing-room for coffee and he took hold of a high-backed wooden chair to bring it forward—and its back came off.

'Here's another old friend and its back still comes off. Why don't you mend it?'

I said it was a job which got put off to another day.

'Well, this is the day. Got any tools?'

So, after coffee, bearing with us the chair, we departed to my sitting-room and started on it.

'Now clearly understand,' he said, 'if this is a success *I* mended it; if it's a failure *you* did it.'

That, I think, sealed our friendship.

But it was not until October in the following year, when they were with us for a long week-end, that we were able to go to a football match. It all delighted him. The dense crowd flowing down the road like a river; the roar of welcome as the rival teams came on to the ground; the shouts of men calling to their player-friends by their Christian names—usually considerably shortened; the staccato 'Aw!' at a mishap (a most remarkable sound from a crowd of sixty thousand); and the deafening roar that greeted a goal. He was much taken with the names of some of the players—particularly Malpas, a famous member of the 'Wolves' at that time. I have known him say when we met:

'There you are. How's Malpas?'—a question I was not always able to answer.

M'in

Mar 12

(189

Dear Miss!

Many thanks for
[illegible] wh: I recd
with joy

Recit
[illegible]

we bang'd the leather [illegible]

After a match in February 1898 he was most keen that I should send him a local paper with an account of it, which I subsequently did. The reporter used a characteristic expression in describing the culmination of a fine piece of tactical work: 'he banged the leather for goal'.

This brought a letter from E. E.[1] by return of post in which he had set the words to music, so greatly did they take his fancy. This letter goes on:

> I have a mug—not the one with the moustache, which you have seen (and heard)—but a brand new one, to drink out of, made at Hanley & presented to me with my name on & an extract from K. Olaf. Yours ever ED. ELGAR.

Late in the afternoon of October 17th, 1896, after a football match, E. E. went up to Stoke to take a final chorus rehearsal of *King Olaf*, which was to be produced at the Hanley Festival a fortnight later. He came back late that night very full of it all; the rehearsal had evidently gone well. He played *Olaf* and other things nearly all Sunday. It was lovely, and I felt a sort of new world opening out before me of which I had never dreamed.

Quite a large party of us—relations and friends—went up for that Hanley Festival and heard *King Olaf*, and I think it was a really fine performance. In the vocal score which I took with me that day, signed by the composer, I put many of the press notices which followed. Some of them are interesting to read now:

> To sum up a necessarily hurried judgement, 'King Olaf' is a work of high importance, one which should turn expectant eyes upon its composer as a musician within whose reach, apparently, lies no common distinction. (*The Times*, October 30th, 1896.)

[1] Most of his friends appear to have alluded to Edward Elgar as 'E. E.'

Generally speaking the cantata surpassed all expectations. It reached a very high level indeed, . . . one of the numerous critics even going so far as to assert that while we have now in this country plenty of composers of great merit, Mr. Elgar is the first among them who has shown distinct genius. (*Staffordshire Sentinel*, October 31st, 1896.)

Fortunately I kept a diary in those days and, still more fortunately, the diaries have been kept. Part of the entry for Friday, October 30th, 1896, reads:

'Mr. Elgar came and saw us in the interval. Went to Choral Symphony in the evening. Mr. E. sat with me most of the time.'

Any one who has sat next E. E. during a performance which he was enjoying knows what it is to be thrilled, and also knows what it is to have an arm black and blue with bruises next day. I have done it many times. With practice one learnt to shift imperceptibly now and then so that the position of the grip varied.

FORLI

THE Elgars were living at Forli, North Malvern, when I first knew them. I think they had gone there late in 1891. On August 17th, 1896, my mother and I went down to Malvern for the day with the Choirmen's outing from St. Peter's, Wolverhampton. We left that party to the care of others and betook ourselves to the Elgars for luncheon.

Forli was a semi-detached house in Alexandra Road and it only took us a few minutes to walk there from Malvern Link station. There was a lawn in front of the two houses divided into two parts—one had a lawn-tennis court, and there was a small tree which gave a modicum of shade on the other. The whole area was supposed to be shared by the occupants of the two houses. There was a fine view of the hills from the front of the house, and the North Hill stood up like a huge hump and seemed a good deal closer than it really was. They had called the house Forli after the Italian painter, Melozzo da Forli, who painted angels playing instruments.

It was a hot day and on the lawn in front of the house was a small bell-tent. E. E., in his shirt-sleeves, was writing at a little table.

'You can't come in here—it's private.'

Hot and stuffy too, I thought, but he seemed to like it. After luncheon he suggested a walk and we spent the afternoon on the North Hill. How lovely it was up there! The wonderful air and the view—I had never been to Malvern before. He pointed out various places and landmarks and I said admiringly:

'You're as good as a map!'

'Better,' he said. 'We'll do the Worcestershire Beacon next time you come, only you must stay, not flit like this.'

He was as good as his word and on another occasion we had another lovely afternoon on the top of the world, 'far away from smoky towns', as he remarked. He soon found that I was as keen on maps and map-reading as he was. Also he added to the interest of these expeditions by bringing in all sorts of stories about the various places that could be seen, and many historical details too. I found him a veritable mine of information. Sometimes he used to tease me by inventing historical 'facts':

'Oh, but surely——' I once began cautiously—

'I wondered when you'd stop me; I thought perhaps you hadn't done any history at your school!'

On March 5th, 1897, I had a letter from E. E. and at the back of the envelope was a red seal about the size of a half-crown.

Forli Malvern March 4

Dear Miss Penny

Here is some locomotive learning; so much nicer than mouldy music.

Alice tells me you are warbling wigorously in Worcester wunce a week (alliteration archaically Norse).

I am very glad, but on second thoughts, as I have never heard you sing I am not sure: but perhaps some day if you are not rushing away I might arrange to show you over the Cathedral organ, K. John's tomb and the Dane's skin: (the Dane is dead).

By the way I have taken to 'die-sinking' as a recreation: here on the back of this is my parcel-post seal: I have to register all my MSS & they will not give a receipt unless

8

'MY PARCEL-POST SEAL'

they are sealed: so I put this on that my works may be Esily distinguished.

Kindest regards to everybody

Believe me Sincerely yours

EDWARD ELGAR

E. E. began to be keen on kite-flying about that time and when they both came to Wolverhampton in the following July we drove over to Boscobel and flew kites in the field near King Charles's Oak. That was a very jolly day. They both enjoyed seeing Boscobel and went all over the old house.

They stayed with us for five days on that occasion and we had music at all hours: *Lux Christi*, *Scenes from the Bavarian Highlands*, and lots of sketches for *Caractacus*. I remember how much I liked the 'Bavarians' and, after he had played the Lullaby (*In Hammersbach*), I could not help interrupting, 'That's lovely—I should like to dance to that.'

'I wish you would: I'll play it again.'

An interruption fortunately gave me time to escape and slip into another frock and also to think out something. (I used to amuse myself by inventing dances rather in the Maud Allan style of later years.) When I got back into the drawing-room peace once more reigned and we tried it out. He seemed much pleased and we did it again, trying bits where steps had not quite fitted in and so on. So much did he like it that I was called upon to 'come and dance Hammersbach' on several occasions at Malvern.

E. E. demanded to be taken over a Rope Walk one day and, when we returned home, played the most comic twisty music till I had to beg him to stop; it made me feel quite giddy.

In February 1898 the Elgars came to Wolverhamp-

C

ton for nearly a week, during which *King Olaf* was splendidly done at Birmingham, and not so splendidly done, alas, by the Wolverhampton Choral Society. I don't know how it was, except that after a brilliant final rehearsal in the presence of E. E. the previous evening all had gone so swimmingly and he had been so complimentary and we were all so cock-a-hoop, that a downfall was about due. These things happen sometimes. The same Society (before my time) had very successfully brought out *The Black Knight* in 1893, and in years to come distinguished itself in the later, greater compositions.

That April I stayed at Forli for nearly a week and had the most hilarious time. There was a Worcester Philharmonic Concert, the first of many to which I went, followed by tea at the hospitable Mrs. Hyde's, in Foregate Street, where I made the acquaintance of many friends, several of whom were to be 'co-variants' (as E. E. called us) of mine: Miss Fitton, Miss Norbury, Mr. Arnold, and Mr. Troyte Griffith. Mr. Griffith came back to Forli with us to dinner that night, but I have in my diary 'Ninepin to dinner' (what impertinence!). It was a most uproarious evening.

I saw, for the first time, the poker-work design over the study fire-place, of which I had heard. I thought it was beautifully done and E. E. was very proud of his handiwork. It was a phrase from the *Walküre* 'fire music'. When they moved to Malvern Wells they took it with them and placed it over the study fire-place at Craeg Lea. It was not taken to Hereford.

Next day we went up to Birchwood, the cottage in the woods, north of the town, that the Elgars had recently taken. It was a lovely spot, though as I saw it for the first time in very early spring its full beauties were not to show themselves to me till later. We unpacked furniture that day and sorted things out.

There were only two sitting-rooms at Birchwood and the study was a tiny place. When a piano, a table, and two chairs were in it there was not more than room to turn round. When they first went up there they had a most comic little old piano. I played a few notes on it and it made a tinny little noise rather like a spinet.

'Surely he's not going to use this?'

'It does sound rather funny, dear Dora, but I assure you dear Edward makes it sound beautiful!'

'That's uncommonly clever of him!'

The next time I went there, however, I noticed that they had changed it for a more modern one—and there was even less room in the study.

In August that year I went to Birchwood for the day with a cousin. She and I lunched with the Elgars and had a lovely afternoon in the woods.

During part of September we were all away from home and my mother had met the Elgars at Hasfield Court, where there was a party for the Gloucester Festival. He took her in to dinner and one of the first things he said was:

'How is my sweet Dorabella?'

'Oh! So it has got to that, has it?' said my mother.

'That's a quotation from Mozart's *Così fan tutte*, don't you know it?'

This piece of information was retailed to me in a letter from my mother, and a few days afterwards I had a letter from E. E. with the musical quotation from *Così* on the back of the envelope. He wrote:

We missed you at Hasfield very much and I could have

made you useful as well as ——— ah! I didn't write the other word. Well: Caractacus is to be rehearsed at St. James' Hall on Thursday at about eleven and my fate sealed at two o'c. I hope your croquet will be good and that you will have the tea service (it is sure to be that) for your very own, and then some Sunday at Whampton you can give us tea and fire eggs at me as of yore.

Believe me, Amicably

Sept. 24. 1898   EDWARD ELGAR

Ever afterwards I was Dorabella.

I had to think of something to call him, of course, and I hit upon 'Your Excellency' as being what I wanted. I think they liked it; anyway, the Lady always referred to him in her letters to me, and also when she spoke of him, as 'H. E.' from that time on.

Perhaps I should explain that I always spoke of Alice Elgar to E. E. as 'the Lady'.

I first made the acquaintance of Carice Elgar at Forli. She was, at this time, about eight years old and had just gone to Miss Burley's school in Great Malvern. She was a dear little girl, very properly behaved and rather prim, and she did try so hard to keep her father in order! It was rather a strain at meal-times as Carice used to stand behind her chair with an expression of patient disapproval on her face, waiting for silence till she could say Grace. Sometimes she had to wait quite a long time, which was most upsetting.

Unfortunately I have kept very few of the Lady's letters, but I remember quite well one in which she wrote most mysteriously about 'some wonderful and most exciting music, dear Dora! You simply must come soon and hear. I have promised H. E. not to say a word.'[1]

---

[1] The Lady used underlining freely in her letters, and those who knew her will understand my use of italics when quoting her spoken words.

On the first of November there was a Philharmonic Concert at Worcester. I reached the Public Hall in time for most of the rehearsal and sat with the Lady. Then we all went to luncheon and, after the concert, to tea as usual with the Hydes. I could get nothing out of either of them about the new music; all he would say was:

'You wait till we get home. Japes!'

At last we reached Forli.

'Come and listen to this,' and we fled upstairs to the study and he played me a very odd tune—it was the 'Enigma' theme of the Variations—and then went on to play sketches and in some cases completed numbers of the variations themselves. No. I, 'C. A. E.', obviously the Lady, and what a serene and lovely thing I thought it; III and IV, both bearing initials of connexions of mine, and as he played I burst with laughter and delight.

'But you've made it *like* them! How on earth have you done it?'

I think he then played 'Troyte', and a roar of laughter followed.

'What do you think of that for the giddy Ninepin?'

After that, 'Nimrod'.

'That must be a wonderful person,' I said. 'When am I going to meet him?'

A voice from near the fire (the Lady had followed us upstairs):

'Oh, you *will* like him, he is the *dearest* person.' (As a matter of fact it was more than a year later when I first saw Mr. Jaeger.)

Then I turned over and had a shock. No. X. 'Dorabella.' Being overcome by many emotions I sat silent when it was over.

'Well, how do you like *that*—hey?'

I murmured something about its being charming and rather like a butterfly, but I could think of nothing sensible to say; my mind was in such a whirl of pleasure, pride, and almost shame that he should have written anything so lovely about *me*. The voice from the fire-place came to my rescue:

'Isn't it beautiful, dear Dora? I do *hope* you like it.'

CRAEG LEA

MY first visit to the Elgars at Craeg Lea, Malvern Wells, was in May 1899. They had moved in about two months before and I had heard much about it. It was a better house than Forli, larger and far more comfortable, and the view across the valley of the Severn was perfectly charming. I was never tired of looking at it, with the changing lights and shadows of passing clouds.

Since my last visit to them at Forli, in November, I had been down for the day to another Worcester Philharmonic, in January 1899, and had had three letters from E. E.

Malvern Feb. 22

My dear Dorabellllla

How many ells long is that? The Variations are finished & yours is the most cheerful; everybody says it is the 'prettiest'—of course intending to compliment the music not the <u>Variationee</u>—that's you. I hope it may be done soon & then we shall have some curious opinions. I <u>have</u> orchestrated you well.

Yrsever

ED. ELGAR

Malvern Sunday

My dear Dorabella

(Will that do?)

Many thanks for the account of the match—it is so kind of you to invite me to anything good, after its over—are you living backwards like the Queen in Alice?

Oh! the fickleality of you.

It is indiscreet of your co-variant (ahem!) W. M. B. to say you are all to be played by Richter. He, R., is to see 'em in

15

Vienna very soon and—if he is not prevented by certain London ——— (mystery!) will play you all in the Spring (tra! la!).

You won't be produced at a festival—dear me! child, the vanity of you!

When shall we see any of you again?

My wife is better
Me   do.
The cook   do.

Yours ever

ED. ELGAR

These dull days (Sundays) the giddy IXpin & Me find nothing to do but to make Peter (Miss Smart's cat) tipsy & send him home about 4.30 in an extremely dissipated condition—we propose it but it hasn't been done yet.

My dear Dorabella   Malvern March 26. 99
How funny you are!

Don't you know yet that 'England' is sufficient address for me?? The idea.

No: I shall not tell: you must find out all about Craeg Lea.

Well: Richter has telegraphed that he will produce the Variations & I think 'Dorabella' is to be published separately as well (of course) as in the set: how like you that!

This is a nice house & a gorjus view: when are you coming to see it: it would be nice to see you again if you don't arrive hot & tired & cross off a tyre-be-punctured bicycle.

A's at church & so shd. I be but I have an untidy eye wh. I am trying to mend: perhaps this accounts for my wild penmanship and then again perhaps it doesn't.

Everyrs

ED. ELG———R

I went down to Worcester on May 4th for another Philharmonic Concert and, after the usual merry tea-party at 21 Foregate Street, went back with the Elgars to Malvern and saw Craeg Lea for the first time. The study was larger than at Forli and, with its exquisite view, really made the most delightful room. I am sure it must have been delightful to work in.

That evening E. E. played the whole of the Variations and played the 'Intermezzo'[1] again afterwards for me to dance to; but I would rather have sat still and heard him play it, I should not have cared how often; the thrill of it was still upon me.

'You wait till you hear it properly played by a decent orchestra; that'll make you sit up!'

Looking through the music and counting up how many of the 'Variations' I knew and how many I had only heard of, I remembered how puzzled I had been by seeing 'E. D. U.' over the Finale.

'Who on earth is E. D. U.?' I asked.

'Well, I should have thought you'd know *that*.'

But I was quite stupid and said, 'I don't know any friend of yours whose name begins with "U".'

'It doesn't begin with "U".'

As he put the slightest possible emphasis on 'begin' my wits at last woke up.

'Oh! of course,' I said rather shyly, knowing that 'Edu' was what the Lady called him—and no one else, so far as I knew. 'It's you.'

'That's a secret. Will you remember?'

Next day we spent most of the morning on the British Camp. We told each other stories of the 'Variations' whom I knew, and laughed aloud about two of them in particular: delightful companions with whom we had both of us, on different occasions, had

---

[1] E. E. said that there was only a trace of the 'Enigma' theme in the 'Intermezzo' which no one would be likely to find unless he knew where to look for it.

such a good time; whose personalities and even little eccentricities had been so uncannily 'reflected' in the music. We also spent a good deal of time that morning going over the story of Caractacus. Walking along the earthworks we imagined Caractacus and his forces going down the hill-side to their disastrous encounter with the Romans, the forest glade where Orbin met Eigen, and the final betrayal of Caractacus and his family into the hands of the enemy. I need hardly say that the story lost nothing in the telling. The whole scene was quite unforgettable. The glorious view over miles and miles of country, the solitude and aloofness of the place, and above all hearing him tell of what had so recently filled his mind—there, on the very spot, the centre of the story.

That afternoon I went into Great Malvern in the brake[1] and chose photographs to put into my copy of *Caractacus*, which was falling to pieces. I had told E. E. previously, in a letter, that I was going to have *Caractacus* bound, and he had replied with a postcard:

> We have awful colds, coffs, sneezes, etc. and are miseries to ourselves & neighbours & hate life. Why bind Caractacus? he was unbound by order of the Czar—Claudius.
>
> In aste   yrs E. E.

That evening I produced the photographs I had bought and mounted ready for the vocal score, and after a good deal of patience and persuasion I induced him to write the title of each under the pictures; but he badly wanted to put 'The British Scamp' (I saw that he had written it on his blotting pad) under the British

[1] A two-horse open vehicle which ran regularly between West Malvern and Great Malvern. The Elgars used to hang out a Union Jack when any one wished to stop it.

Camp picture, and then he tried to put it under his own portrait.

Of that evening my diary says: 'IXpin to dinner. Great larks.' And of the next day: 'Breakfast 7.30. Saw his Ex. off at Malvern Wells Sta. 8.15. Did news-cuttings nearly all day. Home at 7.'

During this May visit I also heard a good deal of *Gerontius*. In June I was there again for a day and heard more. I remember thinking and saying, 'What on earth will an ordinary oratorio chorus do with this?' Most vividly do I remember a third visit, this time to Birchwood, on a very hot summer day. I had bicycled from Wolverhampton, forty miles, and arrived, rather warm and dusty, at the cart-track leading up through the woods to the house. When I was nearly there I thought I would rest, out of sight, and get cool. I heard the piano in the distance and, not wishing to lose more of it than I need, I soon went on. In a moment I came in sight of the Lady sitting on a fallen tree just below the windows. She had a red parasol. I think she sat there partly to warn people off—particularly people with bicycles who had been known to commit the awful crime of ringing a bell to announce their arrival. Leaning the bicycle against a tree, I went and sat down by her without speaking. He was playing the opening of Part II, and those who know the music well will understand what it was like to hear that strangely aloof, ethereal music for the first time in such surroundings. Each time I hear it I think of that beautiful place and that glorious day with the sunshine coming through the lace-work of greenery and branches and the deep-blue sky over all.

Soon, however, the music ceased and a voice behind

us remarked: 'Are you two going to have your photographs taken, or what?'

That afternoon the Lady said she was busy, and we went into the woods and sat down on the ground. After a bit E. E. said: 'If we are perfectly quiet perhaps some one will come and talk to us.'

In a few minutes a robin came, and then a little love of a fieldmouse. It ran towards us in jerks and came quite close, within touching distance, without a sign of fear. Later on E. E. lay down and went to sleep, and I felt very like dozing, what with the effect of my forty-mile ride, the hum of the bees, and the sheer beauty of it all.

'Tank-y-tank-tank', said the sheep-bell distantly. Lo! it was tea-time.

That September it was Worcester's turn for the Three Choirs Festival, and the Variations were down for the Wednesday Concert in the Public Hall: the second performance after the production at St. James's Hall, in June, under Richter. There were several of 'us' there and my mother came down for it too. As she had three relations—brother, brother-in-law, and step-daughter—'Variants', and at least three friends besides, it is no wonder she wished to be present. I sat with W. M. B. and I am afraid we did not behave very well; it was not easy to do so sitting next him as he always saw the fun in everything. He was delighted with 'R. B. T.'[1] and obviously saw the likeness; at

[1] In vol. ii of *Elgar, his Life and Works*, Mr. Basil Maine has inverted the facts in regard to R. B. T.'s voice. R. B. T. had a very high voice, in fact, his voice had never 'broken'. In the theatricals that Mr. Maine mentions, R. B. T. was assuming a bass voice, and his occasional lapses into his normal falsetto convulsed the audience!

the end of it he burst out with 'Well I'm damned!'
When the Finale was over he remarked:

'Well, you're the best of the bunch anyway!'

I cannot remember how many other 'Variations'
I saw that evening, but I think it was a pretty fair
gathering of the clan. It was a splendid performance
and E. E. was right, he *had* orchestrated us well, and
No. X was so lovely that I felt—that first time—that
I wanted to hide somewhere. My sensations when I
hear it now, after thirty-seven years, are very different.
Of all Elgar's music the Variations bring back most
memories of those enchanting days, and the fact that
more than half our number has passed from us often
makes it difficult to keep back the tears.

On November 1st, 1899, I had a wire from Malvern
—'Alice ill can you come.' Fortunately I was able to
go and set off next day, arriving at Craeg Lea in the
forenoon. I found the poor little Lady feeling
wretchedly ill and looking like nothing on earth, but
still up and dressed. I did my utmost to get her to bed
and succeeded early in the evening, and she was really
thankful to be there. As for E. E., he was in high spirits.
The *Gerontius* proofs were arriving in batches every
few days with voluminous letters from Mr. Jaeger,
some of which I had to read aloud while E. E. checked
the corrections, with a constant flow of interjections
and comments.

'What does he say? The crazy old Moss-head! I'm
not going to alter that for him or any one else.'

On one occasion he got up and fetched a trombone
that was standing in a corner and began trying to play
passages in the score. He didn't do it very well and
often played a note higher or lower than the one he

wanted, in fact anywhere but in the 'middle of the note'; and as he swore every time that happened I got into such a state of hysterics that I didn't know what to do. Then he turned on me:

'How *can* you expect me to play this dodgasted thing if you laugh?'

Next day I had little difficulty in keeping the Lady in bed. She said: 'I *do* like hearing you both laugh. Then I know that H. E. is happy and that makes me feel better!'

There were various things the Lady wanted me to do for her in Great Malvern, and when I went in to see her just before starting she asked me to go and find out if there was anything 'dear Edward' wanted. So I tapped at the study door.

'Come in.'

'I'm going into Malvern on some errands for the Lady; is there anything you want?'

'Yes. You. Come in and shut the door.'

'I really can't stop now; I've put the flag out and the brake is almost due—I simply must go.'

'I can't see what is the good of your coming all the way from Wolverhampton if you go and spend half the day in Malvern directly you arrive.'

'You unreasonable thing——Mercy! there's the brake,' and I dashed downstairs and out of the door only just in time. I was lucky in Malvern; I did all the Lady's errands and got back to Craeg Lea in time for luncheon.

That afternoon the Lady had a good sleep. I went out for a short walk with E. E., but we did not wish to be away from the house for long. That evening we had a lot of music, mostly *Gerontius*, Part I, and I did hours of 'turning over', which delighted me.

Then came Saturday and another batch of proofs.
E. E. worked hard at them alone and I did things for
the Lady and sat with her a good deal. She told me
that he had to go up to Leeds on Monday and how
should she manage his packing? I said I was quite a
useful packer and mightn't I do it?

'You can have his portmanteau brought in here,
dear Dora, and I could tell you just what to put in.
Would you do that?' So that was settled and it made
her quite happy.

That evening the proofs, which were nearly ready
to be returned, were put on one side and he settled
down to the piano. I think we had the *Sea Pictures*
all through and sketches and bits of *Cockaigne* as well.
Then he went back to the Variations, and I asked about
the 'Enigma' and what *was* the tune that 'goes and is
not played'?

'Oh, I shan't tell you that, you must find it out for
yourself.'

'But I've thought and racked my brains over and
over again.'

'Well, I'm surprised. I thought that you, of all
people, would guess it.'

'Why "me of all people"?'

'That's asking questions!'

And the remarkable thing is that no one has guessed
it—so far as I know.[1]

On another occasion I asked him again and he said:
'Haven't you guessed it *yet*? Try again.' In fact,

[1] My husband's solution, published in *Music and Letters*, July 1934,
is admittedly plausible and is supported by cogent argument. Neverthe-
less I, personally, have never found it convincing. My own opinion is
that when the solution has been found, there will be no room for any doubt
that it is the right one.

he egged me on to go on thinking till I got it, and I really believe he would have been pleased and amused if I had done so. But as years passed I came to have the feeling that he did not want the solution found, and as time still further went on and no one guessed it he determined never to divulge it himself. He always changed the subject at once if any one began it. I believe that the only two people who shared his confidence were the Lady and Mr. Jaeger.

Then we moved over to the fire and began talking about some of the Variations and how splendid they sounded on the orchestra.

'Why, I haven't seen you since Worcester! Didn't they play well? I saw you sitting next W. M. B.; how did he like it? Do tell me what he said.'

And so we went on and on, E. E. standing with his back to the fire and I sitting in a big arm-chair. Suddenly he took me by my two hands and half lifted me up:

'And how did you like *yourself*, my Dorabella?'

Then I tried to tell him how wonderful I thought it, and how it was far too delicate and lovely for the likes of me.

'Well of course it is! We all know that.'

But I wouldn't be put off and I said how marvellous it was to feel oneself part of the music which had been acclaimed by half the world as being his greatest work.

'You dear child,' he said, and kissed me on the forehead.

Monday morning arrived and I thought the Lady much better. The packing was duly done and the clothes that E. E. was to change into were put ready.

I ordered his cab. He was playing Bach Fugues when I went in to say that everything was ready, and would he go and change?

'I'm not going: I'm going to stop at home.'

I stood doubtfully by the door.

'Oh, very well; but you can bring my things in here, I'll change by the fire.'

I brought them in and departed. The piano ceased for about three minutes and then began again, so, wondering what was happening, I ventured in. Bach was going on louder than ever and E. E. was sitting at the piano in a clean shirt, and trousers.

'You can just do some work and dress me. I'm not going to stop playing.'

How I got him dressed I don't know. I laughed so much I could hardly fasten anything; collar-studs or tie. Yes, *tie as well*; and I made quite a good job of it too. I went and told the Lady how naughty he'd been and I was really afraid she would laugh more than was good for her. At last we sent him off. At tea-time the Lady was so much better that she came into the study and sat by the fire and we did newspaper cuttings all the evening.

I went home next day, and had a letter from E. E. the morning after thanking me for the care of 'our poor invalid' and saying she was much better.

In January 1900 he came to Wolverhampton for another football match, and in the following May I went down for a Worcester Philharmonic Concert—and at last met 'Nimrod'. After the concert we had a most hilarious tea at the Hydes, and went to Foregate Street station on our way back to Malvern. Mr. Jaeger and I became fast friends at once. He *was* a most delightful person. His English was fluent, not to say voluble, but with a strong German accent. He asked me if I knew Gilbert and Sullivan well and we sang 'Oh, Captain Shaw!' on Foregate Street platform while waiting for the train. E. E. in the background remarked, 'Now they're off.'

That journey was one of the noisiest I have ever taken. Our party filled a compartment, and all the way Mr. Jaeger was telling me with great volubility and much gesture how wonderful *Gerontius* was. E. E. was trying to stop him and was calling him a whole string of comic names, and the rest of the party were in fits of laughter.

On Sunday E. E. and Mr. Jaeger shut themselves into the study all the morning. When I came back from church, having called for Carice at her school on the way, I found them still busy, but the Ninepin came to luncheon and it was all most amusing. When they came in to luncheon E. E. saw Carice:

'Hullo, Fishface! quite well?'

'Yes thank you, father.'

'"Yes thank you, father,"' imitated E. E. in a high sort of squeak: and then the unfortunate child was expected to say Grace!

When E. E. was at the top of his form meals used to be exciting. He kept up a running fire of absurd remarks, comments, chaff, and repartee. I have often laughed so much that I could hardly eat and was positively afraid to drink. Also it did not help matters to have the Lady, at the bottom of the table—not always completely approving, particularly if Carice was present—putting in remarks to try to check the flow.

'Oh, Edward dear, how *can* you?' or 'Oh, Edward, *really*!'

'Cheer up, Chicky!' was all she got for her pains.

On this occasion I think the fun was even more than usually fast and furious, because Mr. Jaeger was there and he and E. E. egged one another on. The climax came when E. E. started conducting with a carving-knife!

Unfortunately Mr. Jaeger had to go back to London that evening; but he told me a great deal about his work and promised to send me a copy of his Analysis of Coleridge-Taylor's *Hiawatha* which was going through the press just then and in which he was immensely interested. In the years to come he was very good to me and was a most delightful and interesting friend. He sent me a copy of nearly everything of the sort that he wrote. Some of his letters—brimful of interest, dealing with E. E.'s works as they came to be written—were a perfect delight to me. I kept them all till 1914 and then, alas! in a fit of tidying and re-arrangement, I tore up and burned a huge packet of them. How deeply I regret it now! He sent me several proof-copies of E. E.'s works with the strictest injunction to secrecy. Of course I loved having them and prized them tremendously, but I always hoped most fervently that he would not get into trouble for sending them, perhaps depriving some Important Person of the copy which I hugged to myself at a first performance.

I went with him to a great many orchestral concerts, which was not only extremely enjoyable, but was quite a musical education. What I enjoyed most of all was when he took me to a rehearsal in the morning, followed by luncheon at some restaurant, and the concert in the afternoon. That I usually came armed with miniature full scores seemed to please him very much. He used to say:

'Ha! Very good. That is the way to enjoy the music.'

Many a time he has written and asked me to go up for a concert, and when I had said I was uncertain if I could manage it—much as I should like it—he would reply:

'Now, Dorabella, naughty girl, you must not tease small Germans so!'

It was on one of the first occasions when I met Mr. Jaeger in London—at a rehearsal of the Variations, I think—that I tackled him about the Enigma.

'Now Dorabella, you must be a good girl and not ask me about that. I do not suppose that I could keep it from you if you were to plead with me, but the dear E. E. did make me promise not to tell you.'

'Oh, he did, did he?' I said slowly, 'then I will never ask you.'

Nor did I ever mention the subject to him again. In those early days I always hoped I might guess the secret myself, and the recollection of this little scene with Nimrod seems far more momentous to me now than it did at the time.

The first few letters that I had from Mr. Jaeger were full of comments on *Gerontius* as the proofs came through.

May 25th, 1900. Gerontius grows more & more masterly as it proceeds. It is quite wonderful in parts: mystic, sublime, superb. I have to write a preliminary review of the work in the Musical Times for October, so I am already studying it hard, in Buses, Trains, everywhere. Have it always in my pocket, in fact & go to Bed with it.

We are now discussing the publication of a new pianists arrangement of 'Dorabella' separately and I hope something will come of it. I shall harp on the subject till I have found a good pianist-arranger to make the proper (difficult) P—F arrangement, and till I see the thing in print with a portrait of the original 'Dorabella'. Eh? Fine idea! Send your photo at once!!

June 2nd, 1900.   Dear Miss $\begin{cases} \text{Allegretto } (\text{♩} = 80) \\ \text{G Major} = \frac{3}{4} \end{cases}$

... In Gerontius we have a great, deep <u>thinker</u> & <u>dreamer</u> allying wonderful music to wonderful words, a powerful intellect doing its greatest for a great poem. ... There is stuff in Gerontius that is perfectly beautiful, original & heart rending!

June 9th, 1900.   Dear friend of friend E. E.   He has arrived... and is going to the Götterdämmerung tonight & the Richter Concert on Monday. Why cometh No. X of Variations Op 27 not to that? ...   E. E. has sent the completion of his blessed Gerontius. The work undoes me utterly if I am in the mood. A few friends are coming to my House tomorrow to hear some of it. Elgar, whom I saw half an hour ago, says that <u>perhaps</u> he will come too. The Chorus Parts will not be in the hands of the B'ham Singers for another 3 weeks or more; so your honoured aunt[1] must possess her soul in Patience. I'll send you an advance copy of the Vocal Score for your <u>very</u> <u>private</u> use (mind you: Private!!) as soon as I possibly can. But that will not be for a week or two or three.

... No, the majority of the B'ham audience will not be able to appreciate Gerontius first time; too subtle & original & too mystic & beautiful, but a few like yourself & others will wax 'Wild' with enthusiasm.

September 29th, 1900. In a few days I will give myself the pleasure of sending you a copy of my wretched analysis.

[1] Mrs. Hodgson: a member of the Birmingham Festival Chorus for many years.

I hope your Ladyship will deign to consider it not unworthy of His Excellency's magnum bonum, I mean opus.
(though it is bonum—in fact 'optime'). Mr. Johnstone the
chairman of the Committee (B'ham) told me yesterday that
Richter likes the work as much as I do! If that's so he must
indeed think much of it. I am going to the whole of the
Festival chaperoning a German musician, Professor Buths,
of Düsseldorf, my native town. I hope to see you there
after all.

Then at last came the Birmingham Festival and
Wednesday, October 3rd, saw the production of
Gerontius. My diary says:

'Too wonderful and clever to describe here, but
performance not good.'

I remember well wondering what to put. The performance lacked so much of what one knew was there.
The chorus had not had enough time to learn their
music: the Elgar idiom was like a foreign tongue that
cannot be mastered in a few weeks. It was all rather
dreadful and I felt afterwards that I wanted to get
home quickly and meet nobody. The poor Elgars had
escaped back to their hotel and saw no one—how my
heart ached for him and what he must have felt that
day! On October 15th came a letter from Nimrod
which I quote almost *in extenso*.

October 14th, 1900. I have been 'pitched into' for being
enthusiastic over Gerontius. I don't mind a bit. It was
lack of enthusiasm both in the performers & amongst the
critics which riled me at B'ham & afterwards, when I read
the critiques. Now you Englishers have a composer at last
you might be excused if you waxed enthusiastic over him
for once in a way. But oh dear no! If this were only a
wretched new opera or a dull new oratorio by Mascagni or
Perosi, the papers would have had columns of gossip &
gush about those 2 frauds. But its only an English musician

(not an actress or a jockey or a Batsman) and he is treated like a very ordinary nobody. Oh you unpatriotic creatures. I won't say a word about the performance, but I suffered purgatory!! this disenchantment after my hours of exaltation & refreshment at the Pianoforte was too cruel. I was of course unfortunately placed in a way, for the music was so very familiar to me that I concentrated all my attention on the actual performance, never glancing at the score or analysis. Old St—— the choir-mess-ter ought to be boiled & served on Toast for having had us in Purgatory for nigh 2 Hours. . . .

You ought to come to Düsseldorf (my native place) & attend a Festival (under Buths) to get an idea of an ideal Hall for such a gathering. Such ample corridors, cloak-rooms, Restaurants; and a big lovely garden (with al fresco refreshments) all round the Hall!

All the Germans I spoke to at B'ham (Richter, Dr. Otto Lessman, Prof. Buths, etc. etc.) were enthusiastic about Elgar's work. Directly it was over Buths grasped my hand (coram publico) & blurted out: 'Ein wunderbares Werk; eins der schönsten Werke die ich kenne' etc. etc. . . . To be with Buths for a whole week continuously (except Bedtime) exhausted me, & I longed for a chat with a woman. And it was a fruitless longing. So I say: Where was my co-variation? In Print No. 9 & 10 'were not divided'. Then why in festive Brummagem? I never forgive you that! . . .

Dear E. E. sent me quite a depressing letter last week. I told him it was weak & wicked to write like that. So he replied at once in a better strain. I told him to look at the Introduction & first Allegro of Beethoven's 'Pathétique' (Sonata). That is the mood in which to look adverse circumstances in the face & defy them.

Kindest regards.
Yours sincerely
NIMROD-JAEGER

On November 22nd, 1900, Edward Elgar received the degree of Mus.D. of Cambridge.

During that winter I had six letters from Mr. Jaeger, parts of which I quote.

December 27th, 1900. I'm still trying hard to get Gerontius performed in London, but it is almost hopeless. I still hope Wood will do it. . . .   Yours sincerely

A. J. JAEGER

January 20th, 1901. I think E. is also finishing that Symphony at last. He had the BLUES terribly about 3 weeks ago, but last time he wrote he was joyful.

'Gosh man, I've got a tune in my head' he wrote to me.

January 28th, 1901. [Postcard] Greeting! Variations, not omitting Intermezzo, at Düsseldorf under Prof. Buths on Feb. 7th. I do wish you could go over. Am urging the Dr. to go & hear first performance in Germany. Nice place D'dorf!

NIMROD

February 18th, 1901. Dear Dorabella. Your dear Doctor E. E. is in town & this morning we went together to Queen's Hall to hear Wood conduct the Gerontius Prelude & Angel's Farewell (Kirkby Lunn as the 'Angel'). Oh, Dorabella, the stuff sounded most beautiful, most moving, most elevating. It is the highest thing in English art (musical art) & honestly, I say again it seems to me the noblest, aloofest thing since Parsifal. Wood conducted it with loving care; spent $1\frac{1}{2}$ hours on it & the result was a performance which completely put Richter's into the Shade. I was deeply affected & I felt more than I could express to dear E. E.

April 15th, 1901. By the way, Wood has placed the Elgar Variations in the London Festival Programme. He has just written to me 'How beautiful the Variations are!' At last! Brewer tells me he wants to do them at the Gloucester Festival (Shire Hall). 'We' are getting on, n'est ce pas? . . . The Dr. has just written me a letter in his most Elgaresque style; insults me by saying he would like $\frac{1}{2}$ hour with me, to talk some sense into that German Vacuum! etc. etc. He is a 'killing' person.

April 28th, 1901. Dear Dorabella, I went to the rehearsal on Friday morning and again yesterday when E. E. turned up, and I can assure you Wood makes these things (Variations) hum. I have never heard anything more daringly, devilishly brilliant & boisterous than Troyte or G. R. S., more gorgeous in colour than 'Nimrod', more dainty & graceful than the lovely 'Dorabella'. I sat next M. Colonne all the time yesterday. He dropped in for a few minutes, but he was at once interested & stayed all the time. He was most appreciative, and from being merely interested & saying 'c'est difficile' & 'c'est charmant' he grew warmer & warmer in his praise & more & more astonished, till 'Nimrod' drew from him an enthusiastic 'Ah' & the remark 'it is the best & very beautiful' (He speaks little English) & Dorabella delighted him immensely. 'C'est vraiment delicieux' & similar expressions came from him & at the end (Wood played that stunning coda superbly) he was quite enthusiastic. When Elgar came down from the platform, C took E's right hand in both his own & made him quite a long speech of congratulation. Elgar was quite touched. The orchestra gave him (E) a splendid ovation, I never heard a better one at any rehearsal.

On May 9th, 1901, I went down for the Worcester Philharmonic's performance of *Gerontius*. They did it splendidly and one heard it properly at last. William Green was the Gerontius and I remember how beautifully he sang. Hélène Valma sang the Angel music and she also sang the *Sea Pictures*. We all went to tea at the Hydes'. My diary says: 'Drove up all together from Gt. M. Station, Dr. E. very mad!'

'10th May. Friday. Did cuttings most of the day. William Green is very nice. He stayed till 3. The L. and I drove into Gt. M. with him and came back in the brake.'

When we returned E. E. heard us and called out to

me: 'Child, come up here. I've got a tune that will knock 'em—knock 'em flat,' and he played the Military March No. 1 in D. I *was* thrilled; the whole thing carried one along so splendidly—and as to the coda, I thought it glorious.

'Military March in D this is. What note does it begin on?'

'E flat,' I said.

'Yah! there's a joke! Talk of jokes—what about the trombones here'—pointing to a passage—'they'll have some fun!'

I think nowadays orchestras and bands spoil it utterly by beginning it too fast and taking the Trio much too slow. E. E. played it through that evening in almost strict quick-march time, making very little of the 'Largamente'. Moreover, as it is usually played now, the inner parts of the first section have very little chance.

E. E. came in to dinner that evening in a bright red golf blazer with brass buttons, over his evening shirt.

'I say, you *are* smart,' I remarked admiringly.

'Well, if W. M. B. wears a pink coat at dinner why shouldn't I wear this?'

'A pink coat?' I said, 'he only wears that on state occasions when he has grand people to dinner, like you; when I'm there he wears an old "Ledbury" coat which I like better; it's quieter!'

'Well, I'm not quiet. Far from it.'

I pretended to look under the table.

'It's no use looking. You won't see satin knee-breeches and silk stockings!'

For Saturday, May 11th, my diary says: 'Cuttings again. Miss Norbury to Luncheon & the Ninepin.

EDWARD ELGAR AND A. J. JAEGER

At Hasfield Court, Gloucester, September 1901

Went home 4.20. His Ex. played golf with Mr. Jones but knocked off on purpose to see me off at Malvern Wells. There's a dear for you!'

I do not think I went to Malvern all that summer. The Three Choirs Festival was at Gloucester that year, but I did not go. My people went to stay with Mr. and Mrs. W. M. Baker at Hasfield Court where there was a large house-party for the Festival. The Elgars were there and also Mr. Jaeger. I had letters from both afterwards asking where *I* was. A friend in the party sent me a photograph—not a very good one—of E. E. taking photographs by the porch at Hasfield. He had evidently just taken one of Mr. Jaeger after a bout of singlesticks with one of the Baker boys.

I had two letters from E. E. in October, one from Leeds (here reproduced) and one a fortnight later from Liverpool. The second, dated October 25th, 1901, runs:

My dear Dorabella
   I can't help telling you that the fiftieth person has this morning written (since Leeds—I mean) to know who D——a is & how charming she must be.
   It is so long since I saw you that I forget if you really are nice or if somebody only imagined you to be. So you must come and tell us

Whether you are as nice as

or only as unideal as

Eh? No. Perhaps??

One of the things that always fascinated me in the Craeg Lea study was a collection of books bound in green linen which were piled on a shelf of a tall 'what-not' close to the piano. As soon as I could, after arriving on a visit (making sure that wandering round looking at things did not disturb), I used to gravitate towards that shelf and turn over the green books. He wrote, generally in blue pencil on the cover, the name of what was inside. I remember seeing one fat book with 'Symphony' on it, and I said:

'Are you writing a Symphony? How perfectly splendid! Couldn't you possibly play some of it?'

'Possibly.'

In this way I heard much; odds and ends; bits and scraps; and sometimes a good deal more. It was fascinatingly interesting—I can think of no better combination of words for it.

I have often crept back into the study when no one was about, found a page I wanted, and 'made out' (his writing was not easy) some bit of melody that I wished to remember.

With my head singing with 'tunes' it was very trying to be tackled by friends discussing (and running down) *Gerontius* after that awful first performance.

'There simply isn't a real tune in the whole thing—now is there?'

I tried to say that *Gerontius* was packed with tunes one on top of another.

'Well, sing one of them.'

Of course I sang 'Praise to the Holiest'.

'Oh, well, naturally you take the only possible one.'

Then I sang 'Sanctus fortis'.

'Call that a tune? I don't.'

MIDLAND RAILWAY
Hotels & Refreshment Rooms.
WILLIAM TOWLE, *MANAGER.*

TELEGRAPHIC ADDRESS TO ALL
MIDLAND RAILWAY HOTELS.
"MIDOTEL."

MIDLAND RAILWAY HOTELS.

MIDLAND GRAND.
LONDON.
QUEEN'S, LEEDS.
ADELPHI, LIVERPOOL.
MIDLAND, BRADFORD.
MIDLAND, DERBY.
MIDLAND, MORECAMBE.
HEYSHAM TOWER,
Nᴿ MORECAMBE.

Queen's Hotel.

Leeds.

Oct 15 1907 190

Tell 'em ...
them, ... &
... other people
affectionate ...
(... ...

...)

mesto

To do justice I must say that those very people have, in time, come to describe *Gerontius* as 'very fine', and one does not bully them by asking them what they mean. That they have gone to hear it a second and even a third time is good enough.

I did not see the Elgars again in 1901 until December 5th, when I went down to Malvern for three days. I found E. E. very busy with the 'book' of *The Apostles*. The study seemed to be full of Bibles. He had a Bible open on the table in front of him and there seemed to be a Bible on every chair and even one on the floor.

'Goodness!' I said. 'What a collection of Bibles! What have you got there besides the Authorized and Revised Versions?'

'I don't know; they've been lent to me. I say, d'you know that the Bible is a most wonderfully interesting book?'

'Yes,' I said, 'I know it is.'

'What do you know about it? Oh, I forgot, perhaps you *do* know something about it. Anyway, I've been reading a lot of it lately and have been quite absorbed.'

He appeared to be looking out texts and I offered to help.

'I want something that will fit in here'—pointing to a line.

I thought for a moment and fortunately something suitable occurred to me and I quoted it.

'You don't mean to tell me that comes in the Bible? Show it to me.'

I found the eighty-fifth Psalm in one of the Bibles and laid it before him.

'Well! That's extraordinary! It's just what I want here.'

I think it very astonishing, when one looks at the words which are set in *The Apostles* and sees the immense skill with which they have been selected and put together, that the work was mainly done by one who was finding out the beauties of the Bible almost for the first time. Is there anything more moving, for instance, than the words, and music, of that final chorus?

During that visit I heard a lot of sketches and some of the finished numbers of *The Apostles*—and how I loved the whole of the 'Sepulchre' music, with the beautiful Alleluias! We used to work at the words in the day-time mostly and have the music in the evening.

The Lady had begun to use a typewriter, and as the various pages were finished she would take them away downstairs and type them—she said her slow typing would be very disturbing to us! Her typing was not only slow at that time, dear thing! but rather inaccurate as well.

I was copying out something for him at a table in the window and was conscious that she had been in and gone away again, but I had not looked up. Presently he said very quietly:

'Dorabella; come here.'

He pointed to a page. The words were from St. John's Gospel—very solemn and sacred—in question and answer. The Lady had ended each question with a £ instead of a question-mark. It was so dreadful and yet so funny that we were both speechless. A few minutes later the Lady came back with another page.

'Look, Chicky, what you've put here'—and he handed her the sheet.

CAROLINE ALICE ELGAR

She looked at it and then sat down rather suddenly on the arm of a chair, and the paper fluttered to the floor. Covering her eyes with one hand she felt for a handkerchief.

At the end of this December visit I became the proud possessor of a title! Its history is as follows.

It was during my visit to the Elgars in May 1899, shortly after their move to Craeg Lea, Malvern Wells, that I first saw the Lady struggling with the classification of press notices. She usually wrote at a heavy table with carved sides, one of a number of Indian pieces from her home at Redmarley. This table was a bit high for a writing-table, and she seemed to prefer rather a low chair. As the table was usually covered with letters and papers, almost hiding a large bound blotting-book, she used sometimes to write nearly shoulder high; but this curious position seemed to suit her.

Imagine her sitting thus, with a large news-cutting book open on the top of everything, and piles of newspapers, some whole and some in long strips, programmes, and open letters littered about on all sides.

On the morning after I arrived I found her deep in this work, scissors in hand, and on the floor by her side an overflowing rubbish-basket.

'Are these the *Caractacus* notices? *Do* let me help.'

'Oh, dear Dora, it would be so *delightful* if you could. *Caractacus* and *Olaf* and all sorts of things, and it *does* take up so much time!'

So that was the beginning, and every time I stayed with them I put in as much time at it as I could. However, there was often so much music to be heard and so much 'turning over' to be done and always some one to be amused, that one had not a great deal of time to spare.

'Hullo! *There* you are. Leave all that mouldy rubbish and come out with me,' or, 'What on earth are you doing down here? Why can't you come upstairs and talk to me like a decent Christian?'

The news-cutting business was a bit of a trial to the Lady, I think; she felt that it ought to be done, but she made rather heavy weather of it. I was at work one day and she came in with a large, bulging envelope.

'Oh, dear Dora, I am *so* sorry, but you ought to have had these *long* ago. What *will* you do about it?'

Possibly an interleaving job was less effort to me than to her, but she was quite extravagantly pleased and complimentary at the result. As time passed the work was left to me altogether and I just went on with it as a matter of course every time I stayed there. Finally, in December 1901, after a three-day visit, the Lady suggested that I should take the entire work off her hands and take the book, envelopes of cuttings, and everything home with me and do it there.

Such fun we had over the idea, at luncheon!

'You'll want a truck to take it all away in: much better make a bonfire of it in the garden—pity Guy Fawkes' Day's over.'

'Oh, Edward dear, how *can* you be so dreadful? Dear Dora, *don't* attend to him.'

'You'll have to get an extra rubbish-basket.'

'Certainly,' I said, 'I shall get a washing-basket with a handle at each end.'

'Yes, pitch the whole lot in: it will make a nice bed for your cat.'

But all this nonsense about anything as important—not to say sacred—as the Archives was more than the dear Lady could stand, and she said, *sotto voce*:

'You won't throw away *too* much, will you, dear Dora ?'

So I became, from that day, Keeper of the Archives; and I well and truly kept them for nearly fifteen years.

It was tremendously interesting work and I loved it. It was very exciting getting all the accounts of the various productions and performances (the Lady sent them to me in great envelopes or parcels), reading them through, and deciding which was the best for putting in the place of honour. It was most interesting to read what the different critics thought and the effect that the music had on them. It always amused me to get a bad notice (a rare event), and I usually gave it a prominent place. Specially amusing was it when the writer thought better of it at a later date and hedged.

It used to be rather amusing, too, when I took a finished volume 'home' and left it there in the shelf with the rest. The Lady, dear little person, was so delighted and so interested and would turn the pages over with almost childish pleasure, admiring the arrangement of programmes and pictures with their gay spots of colour brightening the dull newspaper columns. E. E. never looked at it—in my presence at any rate—he just said something disparaging.

'Goodness, what a waste of time! Why, you might have been here all those hours attending to me!'

I was sitting on the floor in the study one morning, sorting libretto typescript, when the Lady came in with an open letter in her hand.

'Dear darling, do you think you could write a little letter to that *nice* Mr. Smith?'

'No, I'm sure I couldn't, Chicky. Have you got page 9, Dorabella?'

'But you simply *must* answer this—nice *kind* little man, he wrote last week.'

'I know he did, bl—— bother him. Well, I can't do it now, I'm busy. I say, can't you find page 9?'

'Yes, but sweet darling, I'm just going into Malvern and I could catch the early post and then he'd have it to-morrow morning.'

'Well, he's not going to. (*Pause.*) Oh, *don't* stand there, Chicky, looking like a stony image! Give me a piece of paper—not that sort, it's too large. Well, what am I to say to him? Dear Mr. Smith—blast this pen——'

'Oh, Edu darling—*please*——'

At this point, though half blind with laughter, I found the missing page 9 and, putting it on the table as I passed, slipped out of the room. As I shut the door I heard him say:

'What's Dorabella crying for?'

It was not always that I found E. E. in high spirits when I went to stay with them. In the years between 1897 and 1912 I went so often, first to Malvern and then to Hereford, that such a thing could not be expected.

'I see you've got a letter from Al. What does she say?' my mother would ask.

'They don't sound very grand. He's low in his mind about something and she seems worried to death. They'd rather like it if I could go down.'

And if I could possibly fix my plans I went.

I was a good deal taken up with both parish and town activities at Wolverhampton in those days; helping with entertainments, sales, and bazaars, and attending countless committee meetings. Besides this I ran my own string orchestra for about four years, and I sang in the Wolverhampton Choral Society, under the conductorship of Henry J. Wood, Granville Bantock, and others, every season for eighteen years. E. E. used to chaff me about the Choral Society, and if I made any sort of criticism he would say:

'What do you know about it? You're only a Chorus Girl!'

Arriving at the Elgars after receiving such a letter I used to find the little Lady looking rather white and tired, and she would say:

'Oh, *dear* Dora, what a *blessing* you've come! Now you will be ready to amuse dear Edward for a bit and I shall be able to get on with some work. I simply *must* go into Great Malvern and do some business.'

The study door upstairs would open:

'Is that Dorabella? Why can't you come up instead of gassing down there?'

When I went up he would say:

'How's Wolverhampton? Come and tell me all about it. Going to football matches is far nicer than all this mouldy music.' Then later: 'Let's go out: have you brought your bicycle?' So off we used to go somewhere.

'I want to be amused, so just make haste and begin.'

It is terribly difficult to have to begin 'amusing' anybody—like turning on a tap—especially when one's best efforts are greeted with a sort of grunt; but

I usually managed to think of something that pleased him and we generally came home happier than when we went out.

The Elgars spent Christmas 1901 in Düsseldorf and there was a performance of *Gerontius* under Professor Buths, the first on the Continent. Mr. Jaeger went over to it with them, and he wrote me a long account of it in a letter dated December 29th, 1901:

We travelled to D'dorf together & had a lovely passage. Buths and a friend met us & we drove to 17 Ehrens Strasse a nice house & a comfortable one. Buths, his Frau Professor & his 2 daughters were as kind as kind could be. On Wednesday morning we went to the first orchestral rehearsal with Soloists. The orchestra of 80 odd was not like Wood's 110 for reading powers or tone, but they answered every purpose & Elgar had not very much to find fault with. Buths, though a man of complete savoir faire is not a great 'interpreter'—I mean <u>co-creator</u>, and there were many passages of which more might have been made as regards mystery, feeling, expression, force, etc. etc. Still, one can't always have everything, & time is an important factor at a Rehearsal. But directly Wüllner opened his mouth to sing 'Jesus, Maria, meine Stunde kam' we said that man has <u>Brains</u>. And by the Olympian Jove he <u>had</u> Brains galore. He made us sit up and realise that Elgar's intention, & what I had expected when I wrote my much maligned analysis, <u>could</u> be realised by an <u>artist</u>. I never heard such intellectual deeply felt singing. Not that W's voice is wonderful. No! But his Brains & his heart are; & they are more than mere voice in a work of such greatness as this wonderful Gerontius. We were delighted & moved to tears. As for dear Mrs. E., you can imagine her state of seventh-heaven-beatitude, with eyebrow lifting, neck twisting, forget-me-not glances towards the invisible Heavens! Don't think I am making fun of her! I am not; but you know her signs of deep emotion over the Dr's music don't you? There was another

Rehearsal with Chorus in the evening. The audience (admitted on payment) was quite considerable & the applause ditto. Buths introduced E. to the Chorus, as he had introduced him to the Orchestra in the mg., and everybody seemed in the best of spirits. Then, next (Thursday) mg., there was another Orchestral Rehearsal when Buths filed & E interfered more frequently to secure readings more in accordance with his conceptions. Then in the evening, the Event. The Hall was crammed full though it was a beastly night (there is no more polite word for it). The Hall is a fine one, and acoustically superb. We (E. Mrs. E, A. Johnstone of the Manchester Guardian, & yours truly) sat in the third row of the balcony right facing the Orchestra and we heard marvellously well. Every little detail came out beautifully & I can assure you I have not had such an elevating soul-stirring experience for years as listening under such circumstances to this wonderful music. The Chorus was perfect, there is no other word for it. The effect of the pp 12 part passages sung dead in tune (throughout the week) was quite ethereal, while the ff tutti were thundered out with imposing force & splendid sonority. They speak of the 'Rhineland tone' among Choruses in Germany & I realised here, where the beauty of the tone lay. It is in a remarkable roundness & sweetness in the female voices & by a big sonority in the male. For though the trousered contingent in the Choir was by no means large, the quantity of tone produced by it was quite sufficient, even for the terrific Dämonen Chorus. That masterful piece, which was so completely ruined at B'ham, was given with perfect ease & yet with strenuous dramatic force which one could not possibly realise through studying the music on paper. Wüllner did not seem in very good voice & he made one serious blunder; but these were only as blots on a summer sun. Elgar was very nearly called after Part I, & during the long pause (20 minutes or more) he held a reception in the 'Soloisten-Zimmer', where I was told many musicians from other towns congregated to congratulate E. & Buths. I alas! was not there, for I was waylaid by my many D'dorf friends who all

45

wanted to shake hands & ask questions & stand me Bottles of Hock which I didn't want. In fact, I didn't want them either, but what was I to do? In any case, I missed the chance of speaking to the 'auswärtige' musicians, as I ought to have done, & wanted to do. So I didn't bless my D'dorf friends exactly. In Part 2 Wüllner was great, especially in the 'Take me away'. The big Chorus 'Praise to the Holiest' which astonished the German musicians by its monumental architecture, was a masterly performance & the Finale, that wonderful Finale, was another revelation to those who heard it only at B'ham. Unfortunately the Angel was anything but angelically perfect. But though Elgar suffered sundry twitches & pangs when the Angel threatened to 'fall', the audience could not have realised, thanks to Buths' alertness, how dangerously near collapse the performance came once or twice through this d—— Angel's shortcomings. (By the way, what the Musical Times says about her, I did not telegraph). Well, at the end E was enthusiastically called, & though he had to fight his way through thronging crowds of people down the stairs & to the front, the applause & shouts were kept up until at last (the time seemed a small eternity) he reached the Podium. There the Chorus & Orchestra & Organ joined in a Tusch & a large fine laurel wreath was handed to him. He asked Buths (so the latter told me) what to do with the thing! Directly I saw the wreath presented I rushed out, took a cab to the Telegraph office & wired 400 words to the Times. Yes, The Times, the account which you read. How it came about that I wired to the Times is too long a tale to tell here; but in addition to doing E & B & the firm a jolly good turn, I earned 20 Marks! Unfortunately, another wire which I sent to the Central News was much mutilated by that agency & only a few papers thought the event of sufficient importance to give the 8 or nine lines to it. So much for the English appreciation of High art in music. If this had only been Dan Leno's first appearance in Germany there would have been columns in all the English papers. Ye Gods! You have to do a lot yet to be considered a musical nation. Your Editors are at fault. After the Concert there was a Supper, but I got to that rather late, because of my work at the Telegraph office. In my absence Buths had made a speech about E, and my inducing him (B) to take an interest in English music, etc. etc. When I came back at last (about 11.15) I was placed between the Angel & her Sister. (I have never been so near feeling good). She, the poor Angel, was <u>very</u> depressed, for cruel, wicked Buths had told her <u>during the performance</u> & after she had missed an important entry, that 'es war scheusslich'. Pretty strong that! I said some nice things about her nice voice (it <u>is</u> a nice voice) & the difficult part & then we became good friends at once. (Of course! you will say.) Well, it was a jolly, most enjoyable evening. Elgar confessed to me he had never had such an one! He made a nice, quiet, modest speech of thanks & appreciation to Buths, Wüllner, & <u>me</u>! & I blushed (tried to) as in duty bound; & at 1.30 or so we at last drove home, having spent an exciting, beautiful day. I wish you & Mrs. Baker & a few other English friends had been there to see how my countrymen, my <u>townsmen</u>, honoured our Doctor. It was everywhere 'Hochverehrter Meister' & 'Geehrter Meister'; E's eyes twinkled thereat. On Friday we were all invited to Carl Sohn's, a rich D'dorf painter. We had a gorgeous feast. Talk about Rudesheimer!! We were 3 hours or so over Dinner, a number of painters & musicians having been invited to meet E. On Saturday Buths, E, Johnstone & myself went to Cologne to visit old Dr. <u>Franz</u> Wüllner, the Director of the Cologne Conservatoire & conductor of the Gürzenich Concerts. He all but promised definitely to produce Gerontius at his first Concert next year. In the evening I sped homewards. I could tell you lots of other interesting details of our delightful stay at beautiful D'dorf, but I must stop. I have sent you a Manchester Guardian giving Johnstone's critique (Very Good!) Next month (February) the M. T. will bring much more about the conspicuous event. The firm appreciate all I have done, the Directors made me nice speeches & have <u>doubled</u> my usual Xmas Box. And now Farewell & say a pretty thank you for this ausführlichen

47

account of our journey. You have never had such a long letter I bet. . . .   Yours very sincerely
RODNIM

The Lower Rhine Music Festival took place at Düsseldorf in May 1902, and the Elgars and Mr. Jaeger went there again for it. There was another splendid performance of *Gerontius* and this time the 'Angel' music was sung by Miss Muriel Foster. The exuberant letter in which Mr. Jaeger told me of her success and of the paeon of praise she drew from Professor Buths is, alas, one of those which has been destroyed. How strange it seems now that the first London performance of *Gerontius* was not till June 1903, when it was done in Westminster Cathedral, the next being at the Elgar Festival at Covent Garden in 1904.

On May 10th, 1902, there was a Worcester Philharmonic Concert, and Herr H. Ettling was tympanist. He was a highly competent amateur. He came with us to the Hydes' and did conjuring tricks after tea. E. E. called him 'Uncle Klingsor' because of his magic arts.
On Monday, May 12th, E. E. wrote:

My dear Dorabella
    Sorry to see so little of you on Saturday. We did not stir today because I am ill with a cold. (Felsnaptha is the moneyback soap) Don't forget this, or me who am
Your inferior friend
ED. ELGAR

Why <u>did</u> you wear the same clothes as last May & May before?

On June 16th I was summoned to Malvern again by telegram. I went down next day and found the poor

BIRCHWOOD LODGE,
NEAR MALVERN.

CRAEG LEA,
WELLS ROAD,
MALVERN.

TELEGRAMS:
LEIGH SINTON.

TELEGRAMS:
UPPER WYCHE

Oct 15. 02

Dear Miss Penny:

(That's not right—).

Dear Mia Dorabella,

(That's feeble)

My dear Dorabella

(pooh! very ordinary)

Now for it —

My dear 'adorable
Dorabellissima

(That'll do)
once more, My

very or most   most or very

My dear Adorable

Dorabellissima!

(Gooh! $2\frac{1}{2}$ a bar

I quite forget what I was
going to say.

Oh!

This is it.

I believe that an association
freehold Gallery of foreign
pictures of Bicycles —

                                    This oh
                                    crony!

        Bismillah!

I am told that a gallery of
                                    loan

- freewheel exhibition for all
Bicycles

(Dear me.)

Look here!

I want to see You!

(No, I don't).

I want to come to
Wolverhampton. Yah!

1. I want to see the pictures

2. I want to see the Exhibition

3. I want to know about
freewheels + if my bike
is worth converting (I
trow not) I will bring it.

4. I want to run in a football
association match

Not the same day.

5. I want food & drink & to decent <u>cigarette</u>

6. I want a coherent reply to this quick

7. I do not want any reflections on the legibility of this letter

8. I send my respex to the house including (unnecessa) the recipient.

9. I kiss your hand from (salaaming) your devoted

little Lady in bed, laid up with a horrid feverish cold. Of course she was fidgeting about E. E., and having some one there to keep him cheerful made her comparatively happy and care-free. He and I had some bicycle rides, and sat by the Severn, and I heard a lot of music in the evenings: the *Coronation Ode* and, of course, *The Apostles*. He wanted to hear all about the Wolverhampton Exhibition and said he should come to it, chiefly, I think, to see the loan collection of pictures at the Art Gallery, and with a view to some of the sideshows. However, he did not come to it, though the Lady and Carice came on July 25th. The day after I left Malvern he wrote:

22 June 02 . . . I have had my tyres 'going-on-into-their-3rd-season'; 1300 miles. Ought I to buy new ones or will these last without

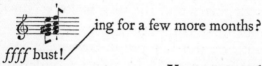 ing for a few more months?

ffff bust!

Yours very truly

ED: ELGAR

P.S. I rode 50 miles (who with?) yesterday without a curse-book out all day. Lovely but lonely. (I was solus.)

His letter dated October 15th is reproduced in facsimile.

It was in quite early days at Craeg Lea that E. E. began to be bothered by receiving manuscripts from budding composers. Later he was really snowed under with them, and he was driven to have a slip printed to the effect that Dr. Elgar regretted that he could not consider any manuscript composition unless accompanied by a personal introduction.

H

49

A particularly dreadful one had come by post one morning:

'Do come and listen to this, Dorabella; you never heard anything like it.'

It was a march song and it had a horribly blatant refrain. After playing it with gusto he snatched it up and hit me over the head with it.

'Oh! come along: let's go out.'

I used to be rather sorry for the people who sent the things, and I said so. I expect they had taken great pains and thought they were lovely. Looking through some that had been opened but not dealt with, I found one which rather attracted me.

'This is really not at all bad,' I said. 'He's got quite a nice melody.'

'Bring it here—let me see it.' He glanced through it. 'It's very ordinary and the nice melody you talk of is straight out of Beethoven.'

'Well, if you put Chopin in *Gerontius*——'

I'd done it now. Afterwards I wondered if I was glad or sorry. I felt that he ought to know what people said, and probably I was the only person who had the cheek or temerity to tell him.

'What do you mean by my putting Chopin in *Gerontius*?'

So I told him of the place which is like the *Polonaise Fantaisie*.

'I know nothing about pianoforte music. I hate the piano as an instrument and I don't care for Chopin and I never heard the piece you mention.'

I determined that I would never speak of anything of the sort again, but on one occasion I gave myself away quite involuntarily. We were going through the proofs of the *Coronation Ode* and he came to 'Daughter of Ancient Kings'. I felt as if turned to stone and I know I went white.

'How do you like that? —— What's the matter?'

I said I thought it was charming, but I knew the beginning quite well.

'What *do* you mean?'

'It begins like a hymn in the Ancient and Modern book.'

'What hymn? I don't know anything about your hymns. Can you play it?'

So I stretched across him and played the first line of 528. 'The likeness only goes so far,' I said.

'Well, I can't help it. I've never heard the wretched hymn in my life.'

'I am quite sure you haven't,' I said; 'it's only a coincidence.'

On December 21st, 1902, he wrote:

Dear Miss

Being a pennytential week, I drop the Dorabella & varying conjugations of it as being worldly & somewhat profane: not that it is as bad as D , or, even, ——: but dear Miss, its not proper for Lent—only this is Advent or something. Yes: Advent. I've just looked it up in the Ency: Brit: (10th Edition 35 volumes) and (and mark you) a revolving bookcase.

(A present! dearie—I mean dear Miss). Persons—the elect—admitted to this Study—revolve 3 times before entering—in honour of (me and) the Bookcase.

Oh! Child, I know things now—35 volumes.

Dear Miss: won't you come & see them? 35 Revolving volumes. Oh! Law! My head goes round.

Dear Miss: it is too lovely for words & its my very own. This is Xmas sirloinidly frivolous—forgive me.

17492

My best wishes for Xmas to you all. I say: dear Miss: I have a Butterfly—alive & flying round the room. He's a beauty & drinks sugar & water at my request & also lives in 35 revolving volumes—I'm off again.

I hope you can read this—I cannot—and you bar the typewriter & it put Dorabellissima so sweetly prettily.

believe me Dear Miss
Yours furtively & revolvingly
ISAAC NEWTON ELGAR (35 volumes)

I only stayed one night with the Elgars in 1903 and that not till late in October. I was ill early in the year and spent most of March and April in Marseilles, at the house of a cousin who was British Vice-Consul. On February 27th I had a letter from E. E. which ends:

> ... & now in haste, a safe journey, a pleasant visit & a safer & pleasanter return to your sorrowing (!?!?) friends one of whom (?which) is Edward Elgar.

On March 21st I had a letter from the Lady—a typed one and a great improvement on a previous effort.

My dear Dora   Craeg Lea   Malvern   18 March 1903

We were very glad to hear from you and that you are there safe and well, it must be very interesting and delightful to see all the shipping. The photo you sent is beautiful, but rather expensive! costing 3 pence extra postage! I have been wishing to write but have been so busy; I really have a great deal to do just now, H. E. is so busy with his work. I do what writing I can for him. Such wonderful things have been written since you were here, and there is a good deal in print now.

H. E. has only been away for Hanley, we had a horrid journey there it took really <u>hours</u>, but the Hotel was very nice and the nice warm hearted Hanley people were enormously excited and could not make enough of 'the Dr.' E. had a splendid Chorus rehearsal the first evening, the Chorus is magnificent, so fresh and spontaneous and seemed to know all the music by heart. E. had no trouble and they took all his 'nuances' at once. Next day Mr. Martin and Mr. Littleton joined us, so all was congenial. At the P. M. rehearsal Mr. Ettling appeared with the Hallé orch. absolutely beaming after their wonderful evening at Manchester.

You know Gerontius was postponed for a week as Coates was ill, we were to have gone, but of course had to be at Hanley on the postponed day. It is of no use to try to tell you all they tell us, you must see the papers, the impression must have been tremendous and they at once decided to repeat it early next autumn. To return to Hanley. First came Froissart beautifully played, then Sea Pictures, (3) and two choruses, and then a reception in the Mayor's Parlour, then back to the Hall and then a most beautiful performance of Gerontius. I think I never heard anything more lovely than the beginning of the Kyrie and so it went on, simply splendid and such enthusiasm.

We returned next day and had hours more travelling.

H. E's new bike came after a month's waiting for it, it looked superb and he tried it and liked it much, went off for a real ride and it all went wrong and has to be sent back. It is so stupid.

He has wretched lumbago today I am sorry to say, I hope it will soon go. We had a good Phil. practice yesterday in spite of torrents of rain, you must come to the concert all being well, and hear the Bavarians, they are sung with such joy. I am afraid I have made many mistakes but I am writing in a hurry and rather tired. I hope you do not dislike a typed letter, but I thought it less tiring to do.

Now, dear Dora, come home safe and well and please look much better.

With love and mind you take care of yourself and not be too 'venturesome', let us hear of you.

Your affecte:

C. ALICE ELGAR (MRS.)!

At the bottom, in E. E.'s writing:

3d to pay! Are you worth it? Much love to the Mistral.

E. E.

September 3rd found me in London for the day between visits to Buckinghamshire and Sussex. I lunched with Mr. Jaeger and went with him to the Hereford Festival rehearsal at the then new St. James's Hall. The gallery was full of interesting people—composers waiting to rehearse their own work, soloists, conductors, and musicians of all sorts. As we came through the doorway he remarked:

'Some one should announce us: "Nimrod and Dorabella!" All faces would be turned this way!'

Mr. Jaeger was of course greeted by all we came near. I knew several people, but many others by sight only. I saw the Lady sitting in the front row. I did not see E. E., but evidently he saw us come in, for I found him behind me when I got to a seat.

'Hullo! What are *you* doing here?'

They were rehearsing the Tchaikovsky Fifth Symphony and there was a pause between two movements. E. E. seemed to like the Valse movement, particularly towards the end.

'Do you know this? You'll like it,' taking a fresh grip of my arm (which was extraordinarily painful) and holding up a warning finger. When the Symphony was over E. E.'s turn came, and we saw him arrive at the conductor's desk to rehearse the Variations. The Lady came and sat by me, full of anxiety and despair at the lateness of the hour, and an almost tragic fear that there would not be time enough for a satisfactory rehearsal. However, all seemed to be well, and it was most interesting and delightful being there.

On October 14th, 1903, *The Apostles* was produced
at the Birmingham Festival. What a difference from
Gerontius in 1900! The Chorus had learnt their lesson
and they did themselves—and the work—justice. The
Town Hall was packed. I did not see the Elgars that
day to speak to, but had tea with them at the Grand
Hotel on the Friday, after the B minor Mass. On
October 30th I went down to Malvern and we had a
glorious evening of music including the *In the South*
Overture. Next day we went to a concert at the
Imperial Hotel and heard the Brodsky String Quartet.
I sat with E. E. and the Ninepin. At tea afterwards
I was introduced to Adolf Brodsky. E. E. took him
by the arm and said:

'Mr. Brodsky, I want to introduce you to Dorabella
of my Variations.'

Adolf Brodsky swung round and nearly dropped
his tea-cup. I entirely forget what he said, or what
language he said it in, but he beamed with delight and
gesticulated with the tea-cup in one hand and a sand-
wich in the other. I really thought he would drop
both.

The Elgars went to Alassio early in December and
spent Christmas there.

In 1904 many important things happened. The
Elgar Festival at Covent Garden took place in March.
Unfortunately I could not go to this or to the rehearsal
for which E. E. had sent me a card. The Lady wrote
me a wonderful description of the Festival—the
Chorus all in white with their pink and blue sashes,
and the masses and masses of flowers. The music was

wonderful and she was delighted with the whole thing.
I had a letter from Nimrod:

37 Curzon Road, W.   27/iii/4

My dear Dora

. . . Why the Beelzebub didn't you come to that unique
Festival? . . . They played you beautifully & the audience
liked you hugely.   They liked me too, though they only
murmured approval, that peculiar audible sigh of approval
which often means more than applause.   They applauded
You, though.   The new overture is beautiful & new, &
shows a surer touch than almost anything else I know of
E. E.'s.   The Apostles impressed me tremendously though
nothing 'came off' as the composer meant it.   The acoustic
defects of the theatre were too great.   I sat near dear Mrs.
Baker, & we twain cried silently & shyly over the marvellous beauties of the various scenes.   You don't consider me
a softy or an old woman, because I can still be moved to tears
by the happiness of letting such beauty 'creep in my ears'
do you?   I say, that analysis of mine isn't a bad guess at
things.   I have without a performance anticipated the effect
& beauties very correctly, though I say so ('cos no one else
does).   Even the 'Guardian' critic, Talbot, after pitching
frightfully into me in October confesses that things sound
quite different now (after he has studied the work, doubtless
with my analysis—read his remarks!)   I smile.   Elgar had a
rare time and everything was splendid.   Ask dear little Mrs.
E.   She must have been in the 7th Heaven of Happiness.
Such swells they met, from the Queen downwards.   A great
time for E. E. & some of us who have believed in him &
fought for him (I had to fight hard for him at Novello's) are
happy.   I have been asked to write a book (chiefly critical)
on Elgar.   Will you help me?   I hope to see something of
you when you come to town.   Meanwhile kindest regards
to you and Miss Danks[1]

Ever yours
NIMROD

[1] Of Wolverhampton.   Then living in Gloucester: a contralto in the
Festival Chorus.

The Apostles was done in Birmingham on April 14th and it was a fine performance. We went over from Wolverhampton and saw the Elgars afterwards. They told us that they were going to Cologne in May for a performance there, and subsequently I had a card from E. E. with a picture of the Gürzenich Concert Hall and a message written all round it:

I know you don't want this, but I send it with much love. The Apostles comes off here tomorrow. Mosshead is here & Alice & I am very hot & want Bier. Yours Edwd. E.

Two days later I had a card from Nimrod:

Dear Dorabella

We had a magnificent performance of the Apostles. The orchestra (150) especially was gorgeous & for the first time within my experience realised <u>all</u> my anticipations (as expressed in my analysis). E. E. was called out after part 1 (a <u>rare</u> honour here) & <u>twice</u> amid great enthusiasm at end. The chorus was excellent & soloists at least quite adequate. Mrs. E. & E. are delighted.

Yours

NIMROD

I went to Malvern on June 15th and reached Craeg Lea in time for luncheon. E. E. and I spent the afternoon on the British Camp and it was perfectly lovely up there. The Ninepin dined and spent the evening, and I heard more about the impending move to Hereford, which was most exciting.

'I've got to go to Hereford to-morrow morning', remarked E. E., 'to do some business: why not come? We might go and see Plâs Gwyn if there's time.'

So next day I saw the new house and thought it most attractive, with its veranda covered with climbing roses and honeysuckle, and its charming garden.

Edward Elgar

We went on to the lawn and E. E. seized me suddenly by the arm and said in a sort of stage whisper:

'Bung yirds![1] Look!' A family of young thrushes was being fed on the lawn under the cedar-tree.

On June 24th, 1904, my diary has just one line: 'Sir Edward Elgar'.

[1] Often, in early summer, when we were out together, he would say, 'Come on, let's look for "bung yirds"!' The sound of the words pleased him.

SIR EDWARD ELGAR
June 1904

PLÂS GWYN

THE Elgars left Malvern in the summer of 1904 and, after a short holiday abroad, settled down at Plâs Gwyn, Hereford. The postcard which I had from Corfu said, 'Come to Hereford and see us soon', and at the end of August I went there for three days. I found the Lady and Carice in possession—Sir Edward was in London—and I went all over the house and was shown everything and found old friends in new places.

'The Indian furniture has positively come into its own here,' I said. 'Doesn't it look nice?'

The study was a fine large room on the ground floor. It had a bow window looking out on the veranda and another window which let in the morning sunshine. When I first went into it I could not help thinking of the tiny study at Forli, and I spoke my thoughts aloud, adding, as we stood there arm in arm: 'Isn't it glorious to feel how he has got on, and how people all over the world are beginning to understand and appreciate?'

I looked round the room with interest; found the 'green books' and other treasures, and I noticed much that was new.

'I think *great* music can be written here, dear Dora, don't you?'

Then we had tea and a tremendous talk about Italy, music, and the Archives; and later on, when we had watered the garden, we settled down to a quiet evening.

That night I had much to think of. I liked finding

them in this nice house. It was larger and far more comfortable than Craeg Lea, and I was glad to realize that things seemed to be improving for them all round. Royalties were coming in more freely and, consequently, ends met more easily. It was so good for them both to be able to go abroad more frequently, and they were making more and more friends every year. In the old days the little Lady so often looked worried and tired, though she never complained; in fact it was always difficult to find out if she was worried about anything special. If any one was tiresome she never spoke of it, and bothers and worries were never mentioned. Once when I was at Malvern I asked how a certain rather tiresome business had been settled, and the Lady drew herself up and said: 'We won't talk about that, I think, dear Dora,' and as she spoke her face became set in an odd sort of way, her large blue eyes staring straight in front of her into vacancy. That was what E. E. used to call her 'stony image' look.

Talking to their daughter recently I was asking about things, and she remarked how difficult it was to find out about business affairs during Malvern and Hereford days, as no mention was ever made in a diary of anything disagreeable or vexing.

After breakfast next morning I heard the Lady in the study opening and shutting windows, and then she came out and shut the door behind her.

'Do go into the study, dear Dora, there's such a surprise in there.'

I wondered if she had been moving furniture and, if so, why she had not asked me to help her; however, I opened the door and went in. I was greeted with a burst of music! But what curious music it was, and very difficult to describe. It was rather like a harp, and the sound rose and fell in arpeggios of intervals of thirds—minor or diminished. It was very strange and rather eerie—in an empty room. I walked forward and saw that one of the windows which looked on the veranda was only partly open and a framework with vertical strings was fixed in the opening. I wondered if it was an Æolian Harp—I had never seen or heard one. The Lady had come in after me and was now beside me.

'Edward loves it. He thinks it is so soothing!'

'I don't think it would "soothe" me,' I said; 'it varies too much; but I call it most fascinating.'

A little breeze sprang up and it seemed as though a second harp joined in with the first.

'That's jolly. What does it do when there is a high wind? I should think it would get tremendously excited.'

'We don't generally have that window open when it blows, and if it gets excited Edward takes it down. The cadences are lovely, aren't they, dear Dora? So ethereal and mystic!'

I had my bicycle with me and I went down into Hereford twice that day doing errands for the Lady—chose some material for curtains, and made them, and also helped with some dressmaking; and the following evening His Excellency came home. My diary says: 'He was very tired but thoroughly cheerful. He brought back a huge box of sweets for her Ladyship from Professor Sandford.'

It was still hot and lovely next day and E. E. and I rode about the lanes on our bicycles. He took me to

Holm Lacy, and we sat in the park by the river Wye and talked about all sorts of things.

'There's going to be some fun in Hereford to-morrow. It's the finals of the Small Car Trials. Shall we go? Fishface will like it, we'll take her too.'

It was rather fun, but in 1904 cars were getting so much more reliable that the break-downs one heart-lessly hoped for seldom happened. I went home that evening—bag, baggage, and bicycle.

On January 6th, 1905, I had a sad little letter from Nimrod: he was ordered to Davos immediately for a three-months' cure. I spoke of it in my next letter to His Excellency but got no answer, though I am sure he thought very gravely of the news. Then, in May, I had a card from Nimrod saying that he was leaving Davos and meeting Mrs. Jaeger at Luzern, adding, 'I am not quite Healed, alas!'

I had had a good many letters and cards from E. E. during that winter on the subject of music for my string orchestra. Some were helpful, some were not, as witness this postcard of March 3rd:

> No, you mayn't, Yes. Yes, you may, No. I think it would be —— No, you may. Yes, you may not. Upon thinking it over I conclude that —— After further consideration I feel that it would be better to —— You might know that my advice is final; please do just as I say. E. E.

I also had a letter dated October 8th, 1904, recommending me to do Handel's 'Water Music'. It ends:

> I like the old Water Music, but I take a little old rye with it now. Yours dispertinently, E. E.

The Elgars went to the States for the first time in

PLÂS GWYN, HEREFORD

CARICE ELGAR ON THE VERANDA

September 1st, 1904

July that year (1905), and E. E. sent me a card from
Cincinnati. On their return the Lady wrote:

> We had a most interesting time, the voyage was lovely,
> I feel quite ready to start again! I have some Yale notices for
> you. You <u>must</u> see H. E.'s gorgeous robes! Dear love to
> all. C. A. E.

At the end of November I went down to Hereford
for a few days and when I arrived the Lady met me
in the hall. I thought she looked very grave and I
wondered what bad news she was going to tell me.

'Dear Dora, it *is* nice to see you, but H. E. is *very*
busy and I am afraid you'll have a very dull visit!'

I felt for a moment that she would have been thankful if I had said I would go straight back home there
and then; but I didn't say it. Instead I said:

'That's all right! I expect there are heaps of things
I can do for you, and if he is busy I can keep you
company.'

She seemed a little happier at that and took me
upstairs. 'He's hard at work on *The Kingdom*—he's
been in the study all this morning and he only had a
mouthful of luncheon! I've heard *wonderful* strains
every now and then and it's all such beautiful and
exalted music!'

I was pretty sure that she was trying to impress me
with the wonder and importance of it all; she feared
that my visit might be a distraction to him, and this was
a hint to me to keep in the background as much as
possible.

I said something appropriate showing that I understood, and she cheered up a bit more.

'Well, make haste and come down, dear Dora. Tea
will be ready soon. You remember that when H. E.

is busy like this I *never* have a bell rung for meals and we are all as quiet as possible!' (More hints!) I had been with them, of course, at other times when he had had what I irreverently called 'a composing fit', but this one promised to be the best—or worst—that I had experienced so far. The Lady and I had a cosy tea by the fire and had much to say. During tea she filled a thermos flask with tea and put it on a tray that was all set ready, and I noticed that there were eatables in covered muffin-dishes. I sprang up to open the door —I knew it would be useless to offer to take the tray— and she put it down on an oak chest outside the study door. She came back and we finished our tea. 'If H. E. opens the study door he'll see the tray and take it in.'

But no door was opened and no tea was taken in. There was just silence.

I had brought some needlework and I fetched it, and we talked about what I could do for her next day; and so the time slipped away and we went up to dress for dinner.

Dinner was just coming in and the Lady was in the hall when the study door opened and E. E. appeared.

'Where's dinner?' he said rather roughly.

'It's here now, dear darling—we are just going in.'

He looked up and saw me on the stairs:

'Hullo, you here? I'm busy.'

'Yes,' I said, 'so I hear. I'm keeping the Lady company.'

We went in and had our dinner. He never spoke. When he was not looking at his plate he looked straight in front of him with rather a tense expression. He was very pale and looked tired and drawn. Half-way

64

through dessert he pushed his chair back, hit my hand, which happened to be on the table, quite sharply, and left the room. He banged the study door and turned the key. For an instant I thought, 'That's to keep me out!' I looked at the Lady inquiringly.

'He always locks himself in now that the study is downstairs,' she said, 'he feels safer!'

As a matter of fact I never, in all the many times I stayed with them, went into the study unless I was asked, or sent, or unless the door was open.

'Oh, *dear* Dora, look at your *poor* hand! That *was* naughty of Edward, really!'

'It looks much worse than it is,' I said, rubbing it, 'I expect it will be all right soon.'

So we went back to our drawing-room fire, and then began one of the most remarkable evenings I have ever spent.

'Don't you think,' I said, 'that he looked, during dinner, as though he were listening to something far away?'

'What a nice idea, dear Dora! Yes, I do think so.'

Coffee came in and the thermos on the tray was emptied and washed and filled with coffee. I had mine good and strong: I wanted to keep awake. We sat on, talking, reading, working, and when 10.30 came the Lady said:

'Oughtn't you to go to bed, dear Dora? I'm sure you're tired.' But I said please mightn't I stay up with her, I should so much like to. So she said no more about that, for which I was thankful. Presently she said:

'Don't you think it would be nice to make ourselves some tea?' I went with her to the kitchen, and there was a tea-tray all put ready and a large plate of sand-wiches covered over, and plates of cake and biscuits. 'It isn't the first time this has happened,' I thought, and carried the tray of eatables into the drawing-room. We had two sandwiches each and took all the rest to the tray on the oak chest.

While we were drinking our tea we heard the piano at last! The fire-places in the drawing-room and study were back to back and the sound seemed to come down the chimney. As the house was all quiet we heard quite well and we just sat and listened, and forgot the time. It was really most wonderful hearing the scene as it grew, phrase by phrase: once a reminder of some-thing in *The Apostles*—the Lady and I looked at one another—and then it was all new again.

I don't know how long he went on playing, but silence came at length and we both realized that it must be very late and that we were greatly in need of another brew of tea. I went out and made it this time, and the hall clock struck half-past one as I passed it. He was playing again when I came back with the tray, but we had not finished a first cup when the music stopped. We heard his key turn, and the Lady got up and opened the drawing-room door.

'Hullo! You still up? and Dorabella too? and tea! Oh, my giddy aunt! This is good!'

I went and fetched in the other tray and we had a grand meal. He was himself again—quite different from what he had been at dinner. He looked tired, as though he had been through some ordeal, but the ordeal was now over and one could feel what a relief it was.

After we had drunk up all the tea and eaten all the

sandwiches and most of the cake and biscuits we went into the study. 'Come and turn over, Dorabella, will you?' and he showed me where part of it was on the back of another page and that sort of thing. Then he played the whole of that evening's work, and more, straight through, and we recognized passages we had heard down the chimney. I saw the words, 'The sun goeth down; Thou makest darkness, and it is night...' When I hear *The Kingdom* now how can I help remembering that evening?

It was well after 2.30 a.m. when I made a move to go to bed.

'I think we'll all go now, dear Dora'—the Lady got up—'I must just go and put things straight in the drawing-room.'

Seeing me make for the door, E. E. called out:

'Oh, do stop and talk to me, Dorabella, I haven't heard half the news yet.'

'Yes, *do* stay, dear Dora, and talk to him; I *promise* not to carry any heavy trays!'

He opened the door for her and I remember the sound of her quick little steps going across the hall.

'Fancy your staying up all that time—why ever did you?'

'I just loved it,' I said.

'You do look charming in that frock. When I saw you on the stairs——'

'I wished I'd brought something quieter and more ordinary, but you see I never bring——'

'Don't you dare to bring any dingy, smoky frocks when you come to stay with me, because I won't stand it——and you only looked at me twice during dinner!'

'Twice, was it? Well, I was terrified! I simply daren't look at you for fear of putting you off your stroke or something.'

'At first I hoped you wouldn't and then, as dinner went on, I hoped you would. Finally I went away; you'd won, and that was why I hit your hand so hard. Did it hurt? I meant it to!' He picked up my hand and inspected it.

'It stung a bit at first, but there doesn't seem to be a mark. Well, I'm off. Do you know that it's nearly three to-morrow morning?'

The following day I heard more of *The Kingdom* music. E. E. worked alone all the afternoon, and after tea I helped him with sorting papers in the study.

We heard the postman come and I went to see if there were letters for either of us. The Lady was in the hall.

'One for you, dear Dora, and some dull things for H. E. Will you take them in?'

'What's all that rubbish? I can't be bothered with it.'

'Shall I see what they are?'

Most of it was easily disposed of, but I stared at the last one in silence.

'What have you got there?'

'It's from a Temperance Society,' I said. 'They want you to join, and the Secretary encloses a card for the coming season.' Hardly able to speak for sheer joy I put the card down in front of him, adding, 'They've chosen a good motto for their Society, haven't they?' Printed in old English lettering at the top of the card was 'Hold Thou me up and I shall be safe.'

'That's from the Psalms, isn't it?'

'Yes,' I said, 'the hundred and nineteenth.'

'Could you believe it?' he began—and then I'm afraid we simply exploded with laughter!

I have never known him more delighted with anything. Hearing the noise the Lady came in to know what was the matter. Holding out one hand to her and flourishing the card in the other he called out:

'Come here, Chicky dear, and see what they've sent me!'

The Elgars spent Christmas, 1905, in England, and I had a Christmas card from him from Hereford.

I had sent him a programme of one of my concerts and had a reply dated February 18th, 1906.

My dear Child

Many thanks for sending unworthy me your beautiful programme: I have only found, with Troyte's help, fourteen mistakes. I hope all went well and you are happy over it. I should have enjoyed myself—I am not saying anything about the concert—if I could have incogged* (!) myself into the Baths Assembly Rooms for the occasion. My best benison on you and your Orchestra.

Yours very sincerely

EDWARD ELGAR

* new & useful verb!

The cold of the winter in the Black Country was always rather a trial to me, and I went up to Cumberland on March 12th for a fortnight's change. The entries in my diary during that visit have the word 'Archives' against most days. I remember that I had got rather behind with the work and I took the whole thing—book, parcels, envelopes, and all my paraphernalia—with me. My kind hostess put a table at my disposal which was carried from room to room wherever I wanted it with everything on it undisturbed, and it was covered over with a cloth at night. That was luxury and I got on famously.

Now that the Elgars had left Malvern I did not stay with them nearly so often. Hereford was much farther away and, though not beyond reach by bicycle, the return journey next day, which I had sometimes done from Malvern, would now have been rather an undertaking. I think also that E. E. must have severed his connexion with the Worcester Philharmonic, as I have no record of going to one of those concerts after 1903, and there were no longer, therefore, the opportunities of meeting the Elgars on those delightful days and going back with them afterwards.

The Birmingham Festival of 1906 began on Tuesday, October 6th. There was a glorious performance of *The Apostles* on the Tuesday evening and I saw no empty seat in the Town Hall. The soloists were fine—Agnes Nicholls, Muriel Foster, John Coates, William Higley, Ffrangçon-Davies, and Andrew Black! On Wednesday morning we had *The Kingdom*. My diary refuses to make any comment beyond, 'Splendid performance'.

I am afraid I always felt terribly on edge at these first performances of His Excellency's works. I really knew so much of them beforehand and was so anxious that the performance should be as he wished that to sit surrounded by people who criticized without knowledge and made comparisons which only ignorance of the music could account for was exceedingly trying!

Next day the Lady spent the afternoon with us at Wolverhampton and we heard all the news. They had been delighted with the performance of *The*

Apostles and *The Kingdom*. We talked about the 'Chair of Music' at Birmingham University and the lectures that His Excellency was giving there and heard many tales of the visit to the States.

In the spring of 1907 I spent six enchanting weeks at the Italian Lakes and was at Caddenabbia for Easter. On my return home I found a card from Cincinnati awaiting me. The Elgars had gone to the States early in April and were there for some time. I did not see them again that summer and had no letters from His Excellency, but I probably heard from the Lady, and again I deplore that so many of her letters have not been preserved.

I was having very sad letters from poor Nimrod. Every winter he was forced to leave England, his family, and his work, and go abroad for treatment. He used to get terribly depressed and downhearted and one began to dread that his health would never be any better. If only he could have stayed on at Davos in 1905 and given the cure a real chance, instead of coming home in May, all might have been well. I had a card from him dated April 18th, 1907, from Dr. Brackmann's Sanatorium, Lippspringe, Westfalen:

Many thanks for your kind letter which has been forwarded to me at the above address, where I hope to stay for two months or so. I'm delighted to hear you feel well after your splendid Holiday. Strange! I very nearly went to the Italian Lakes. What a joke if we had met and Oh, what a surprise! I'm here to drink the waters which are supposed to do the lungs good. Nous verrons! I came via Munich, where I spent 3 days (& heard the Joachim quartet—poor Joachim. He really can't any longer.) I liked München muchly & had a nice time, though quiet (very) naturally.

When I'm allowed to by my Dr., I'll write you a letter. Meanwhile be a good child & send me the promised continuation of your delightful screed. Ever yours,

NIMROD.

If I could do nothing else for him I could at least write and tell him everything I could think of which might amuse him, and finding that it did so was reward in plenty.

In September, 1907, I went to the Gloucester Festival and stayed with Mr. and Mrs. Danks for it. *The Apostles* on Tuesday evening and *The Kingdom* on Wednesday morning were both very well done. I met the large house-party from Hasfield Court which included my mother and Mrs. R. B. Townshend. I had an invitation for myself and two friends to a luncheon given at Beaufort House by the Gloucester Wagon Co. Amy Danks was one of my guests and the other was an aunt, Miss Helen Heale, who had come up from Ross specially to hear *The Kingdom*. In the luncheon interval we saw His Excellency and the Lady and I introduced my guests. I also met Mr. Leo Schuster that day. Speaking of the Shire Hall Concert that evening my diary says: 'Rather dull programme except for Plunket Greene singing Stanford's *Songs of the Sea*. Sat next Mrs. Ludovic Goetz.'

On Thursday my diary says: 'Luncheon again at Beaufort House & saw Hasfield party. Amy & I went to tea at the Brewers'. The Elgars were there and hosts of people. It was great fun. Mr. Atkins teased A & me about the programme for Worcester pretending that he had all sorts of novelties in prospect— which he hadn't! Went to the Lobgesang in the evening & said Goodbye to the Elgars afterwards.'

72

After the Festival I went down to Devonport for a week to stay with Naval friends and then on to Hereford on September 20th, to find the Lady and E. E.'s niece, Miss Grafton, alone at Plâs Gwyn. His Excellency had been kept in London. I went home next day and had a letter from him:

The Athenæum   Pall Mall, S.W.

21 Sept. 1907

My dear Dorabella

I am so sorry that the exigencies of my professional duties —— gosh!

Look here: I couldn't very well manage to come away from town & missed you: this is sorrow, but of a chastened description as I shall see you soon, of course: that's all.

Anyhow the Gloucester vision ought to last you for years.

Don't be silly—me I mean.

Kindest regards to the Rectory

Yours sincerely

EDWARD ELGAR

On October 16th His Excellency and the Lady came to tea with us at Wolverhampton. There was a concert that night at Birmingham and they came to us when the rehearsal was over. I did not go to the concert. How we talked! The Lady and my mother naturally had much to say and I had much music to hear.

I stayed in London for a few days in December and spent the afternoon of the 13th with Nimrod at his house at Muswell Hill. I was terribly sad and shocked at the change in him and it was a very great effort to me to forget it and try to be amusing and cheerful. I could not help realizing that the end was fast approaching. Dear 'Small German' (as he used to call himself), what a tragedy this was! Such a brilliant brain and such quick wit and understanding of people

L

and things, such fine enthusiasm for genius, expressing itself in a torrent of words! I had to do my full share of the talking that day though, as it made him cough and it was a cough that shook him.

If I am to believe my diary I only saw the Elgars on two days in 1908 and had not a single letter from His Excellency. I had an Easter card from Rome where they were for a few weeks.

On April 3rd I had a letter from Nimrod. After saying how ill he had been he cheered up a little:

> One of the letters I did manage to write was to Elgar who sent me the proofs of his five new part-songs, which I suppose you have seen by now? They are splendid, are they not? The first one, 'There is sweet music here' is an exquisite conception, a perfect Gem, a masterpiece worthy of E. at his best. . . .
>
> I wrote Ivor Atkins a card the other day asking about his programme for the (Worcester) Festival. He wants to do Debussy's 'Après-midi d'un faune'! Oh! if the 50,000,000 Worcester parsons knew the lewd, impossible <u>poem</u> on which this music is built! There would be an outcry and a show of Holy Horror! Debussy is a thorough Décadent &, well—he must be a pig to choose such a poem to be inspired. Music is coming to a fine pass to need such crutches to keep it going. All the same I like the piece—as music—very much.
>
> I say, what <u>is</u> Elgar composing now? You, as Keeper of the Archives <u>must</u> know, surely. He never tells me now, the wretch. I am glad you are coming to London soon. Ja! I <u>do</u> hope you will come and see me. I will try if the weather will let me—to get a little stronger by then & so we can have a long chat.
>
> Ta Ta. Very sincerely yours
>
> A. J. JAEGER

I went to Ireland in August 1908 for a month and returned just in time for the Worcester Festival. I went down on the Thursday and lunched, in the interval, with the Elgars. I heard all about the Symphony being finished and ready for the production in Manchester on December 3rd and that it was to be done at the Queen's Hall and at Hereford soon after.

I could not go to any of these performances, alas! but I was delighted to hear from Nimrod that he had been at the Queen's Hall, having been 'fetched, by a kind friend, in a motor cab all the way from Muswell Hill'. He wrote:

How I wish you had been there. I never in all my experience saw the like. The Hall was <u>packed</u>; any amount of musicians. I saw Parry, Stanford, E. German, J. Corder, E. Faning, P. Pitt, E. Kreuz, etc. The atmosphere was electric. ... After the first movement E. E. was called out; again, several times, after the third, and then came the great moment. After that superb Coda (Finale) the audience seemed to rise at E. when he appeared. I <u>never</u> heard such frantic applause after any novelty nor such shouting. Five times he had to appear before they were pacified. People stood up and even <u>on</u> their seats to get a view. As regards my impressions, I <u>must say</u> I was delighted. The lovely Heavenly Adagio reduced me to tears. The Scherzo both amused and charmed me. The Coda is superb and winds up the symphony in a blaze of glory. That Coda is <u>quite new</u> in laying out and effect. On the whole a splendid & noble & <u>highly individual</u> work, full of the most lovely detail work & any amount of Brains & Heart. ...

I went on Saturday too & took my wife & we enjoyed the work immensely. The House was packed again, & Busby, the managing Director of the Symph: Orch: Co. told me the day was a <u>record</u> for them in the way of selling tickets. ...

Yours

NIMROD

75

On December 9th I went down to Worcester for a concert at which the Brodsky Quartet was playing. I did not keep the programme and I cannot remember anything about the afternoon except that I had tea with the Elgars and the usual party of friends afterwards, and that I met Dr. G. R. Sinclair for the first time. He and I travelled back as far as Birmingham together—he was Conductor of the Birmingham Festival Choral Society and was due there that evening for a rehearsal.

We talked of many things; including music, and bulldogs! I had heard of Dan and of his fall into the Wye[1] and we speculated as to whether he was the only dog immortalized in music. I heard of his devotion to, and unwillingness to leave, his master, and that he was a regular attendant at the Hereford Choral rehearsals.

'What does he do while you are taking rehearsals?' I asked.

'He lies under my desk and sometimes gets kicked by accident, but he does not seem to mind. The thing he cannot stand is people singing out of tune; then he growls. Once the tenors sang so flat that I had to turn Dan out.'

'*What* a reflection! Fancy being told you sing flat enough to turn a dog out! I'm thankful it wasn't the sopranos, anyway.'

Birmingham was reached all too soon and we went our several ways: he to his rehearsal and I to continue my journey home. Thus I made another 'Variation' friendship.

The Elgars spent Christmas 1908 at home and on January 7th, 1909, I went to Hereford for a couple of days.

---

[1] The opening bars of Variation No. XI, 'G. R. S.'

I had been to hear the Symphony at the Queen's Hall on January 1st with two friends, and I went home with them to Rochester for a week, and then on to Hereford. That first evening at Plâs Gwyn we had much to say about the Symphony: the splendid performances: three since the production at Manchester on December 3rd! I told them how delighted dear Nimrod was with it and how he had written me a huge long letter all about it. I thought they both looked very grave and the Lady changed the subject very quickly. Afterwards I heard that they had both been so dreadfully shocked and grieved to see such a change in him that it had rather upset them. I don't wonder. It is really amazing that he managed to go to Queen's Hall, even by 'motor cab', and enjoy it.

'I am sure it was an immense pleasure to him to be there,' I said, 'and he can have so few pleasures now.'

On April 24th there was a very fine performance of *Gerontius* at Queen's Hall to which I took five friends. I think only one of them had ever heard it before, so it was rather an occasion.

The Elgars went to Italy early in May and I had a card from him at Careggi, Florence, dated May 4th, 1909.

On May 19th I had a letter from Mrs. Jaeger telling me of her husband's death and giving me his 'Goodbye' message. So it had come at last, and Nimrod had passed on.

It was when I went down to Hereford in August 1909 that I found another person installed at Plâs

Gwyn—a turtle-dove. It had a large wicker cage in the veranda, but the door was always open and the dove came and went as it liked.

I remember well arriving after an exceedingly hot and dusty railway journey. The house felt beautifully cool and there were flowers everywhere. I came downstairs after a welcome wash and change and I saw that the study door was ajar. Pushing it open a little I just caught sight of a vision and though I instantly 'froze' I was too late, the dove had seen me and was gone. E. E. was at his writing-table and the dove had been sitting on the stationery cabinet in front of him. His Excellency looked up and saw me.

'There you are. Did you see Dove? I wish she wouldn't sit there. She sits and watches my pen every time I want more ink. I know she'll put her beak in the inkpot one day.'

'New and interesting variety of dove,' I said. 'The inky-beaked turtle-dove.'

'Look here, I'm trying to write a letter. I can't think how you expect me to write sense.'

'I never expect ——' There was Dove on the window-sill! Would she come back? Standing motionless by the table looking at some music seemed to be a reassuring attitude in a stranger, and in she came. She perched on the pole of the library steps and sat there looking at me, first with one eye and then with the other.

'If you'd stay a decent time and not flit as you always do she'd soon be all right,' E. E. said very quietly.

'Well,' I said unwisely, 'I'm staying three whole days this time.'

'There's Alice ringing the bell for tea and I've not

78

SIR EDWARD ELGAR

Taken in 1909 by Miss May Grafton at Plâs Gwyn,
Hereford

finished this writing. If only Alice wouldn't ask visitors whom one doesn't want—O my unhappy gizzard! *Do* go away—Dove's gone long ago.'

Tea was set out under the great cedar on the lawn and there was the Lady, looking lovely and cool in a blue frock, arranging comfortable chairs. The garden was gay with flowers and the veranda was half smothered with climbing roses. Butterflies danced along the borders in the sunshine, and close to us, in the cedar, sat the Dove. She had much to say, but after tea we sat silent; it was all so lovely.

Then I heard more about the Dove.

'She led me a fine dance in the spring,' E. E. said. 'I thought she seemed out of sorts, but I did not guess at once what was the matter. She used to wait till I was near the cage and then go into it and sit down on the floor. I believe she wants to make a nest! I said to myself; well, why doesn't she do it? Next day I found her in the veranda struggling with a great stiff straw. She flew up with it over and over again trying to get in through the cage-door. At last she got it in and proceeded to sit down on it in a helpless sort of way and she looked at me with such a reproachful expression! I wondered what she wanted me to do. "You absurd thing," I said, "you can't expect me to show you how to make a nest?" But evidently she did; so I went round the place looking for things—feathers, bits of hay, leaves—Dove watching me all the while and never very far away. Of course I didn't trouble to arrange the stuff, I just put it down in a little heap on the floor of the cage and thought she'd use the nesting-box, but not a bit of it! There she was next morning, sitting on it just as I'd put it—and she'd laid an egg!

No, there were no bung yirds! Dove was a bad sitter; pity, wasn't it?'

That evening we watered the garden (E. E. was quite good with a hose) and then we sat out until it was nearly dark. We visited Dove, who had long ago retired for the night, and then we settled down to music.

I think I heard nearly all the Violin Concerto that evening, and how I loved it, every bit of it, from the beginning. What sadness and regrets; what high hopes and what dreams was he describing? Later, of course, I saw the dedication and guessed the rest.

Next day and the day after were both gloriously hot. We breakfasted out on the lawn under the cedar, in fact we had all our meals out, closely attended by Dove. His Excellency was busy and worked indoors the first morning, and I wrote letters at the table under the cedar. Dove was rather worried about it. She sat near me for a bit and then flew over to the house and I saw her disappear through the study window. She would be there for a short while and then come back again to me; in fact, she spent the whole morning going to and fro. How I wished I could understand what she was saying as she bowed and curtsied. She *was* a darling!

Next day a batch of proofs came from Novello's and I unpacked them. It seemed so dreadful to have no exuberant letter from dear Nimrod and I spoke of it.

'Don't talk about it. It's too sad. I can't bear it.'

But that evening, sitting in the study—the Lady having said 'Good night' early and departed to bed— we talked much about him. I told E. E. how I had spent the whole afternoon at Muswell Hill the previous winter; how I had tried my utmost to cheer him, and how I had cried most of the way home in the train afterwards.

The Elgars had rather a hectic time of it at the ensuing Three Choirs Festival at Hereford. They were looking forward to having a jolly house-party for it at Plâs Gwyn, but Carice upset all their plans by developing scarlet fever. Nothing daunted, however, they took Harley House, in Hereford, and had their party there. The story of what happened about the lack of bells is vividly described by Mr. W. H. Reed in his book, *Elgar as I knew him*. The bedrooms at Harley House were not fitted with bells and E. E. raided a Hereford toy-shop for all sorts of things that would make a noise and these were hung up outside the doors. I should think there were no straight faces among the domestic staff during that Festival.

The Birmingham Festival was in October, and on the Tuesday evening we had a fine performance of the Symphony and on the Wednesday morning we had *Gerontius*—both conducted by Hans Richter. Birmingham really heard *The Dream* this time. I saw His Excellency at both concerts, but did not speak to him.

On November 25th I went to Oxford to stay with Mr. and Mrs. R. B. Townshend. There was an orchestral concert at which the Variations were to be done and R. B. T. wanted to go to it with me. Poor thing! I'm afraid he was rather bored—he was entirely unmusical—but he was entertained by what I could tell him of the other 'Variations' and amused by my 'explanatory notes' on the subject of his brother-in-law, 'W. M. B.'

'E. E. called you the "Delight-maker", didn't he ?'

'Yes; that was after those theatricals when I did the old man. Those *were* the days!'

He wanted to know why W. M. B. was amused and why he said what he did at Worcester after the 'R. B. T.' Variation, and in what way I thought it was like him. This was a little awkward for me as I could not very well tell him how wickedly like him it was, with all his funny little eccentricities and ways of speaking. However, I told him what I could.

'That's no end interesting,' he said, 'but I wish I could see it just as you do!'

I do not appear to have had a Christmas card from either E. E. or the Lady, but I received a crazy letter from him dated January 7th, 1910. He seemed to have been in a very good humour when he wrote. On the back of the envelope was his new seal, not, this time, of home manufacture.

On January 24th I went up to London for the Jaeger Memorial Concert at the Queen's Hall. I found it rather a trying experience, particularly the Variations. I noticed, however, that others found it 'trying' besides myself. I was glad to see that the Hall was well filled and I wondered, looking round before the concert began, how many of those present had really known him personally. It was a fine tribute to the memory of the great 'Small German' who had done so much for English music.

In the following April I went abroad—to Florence this time. The evening before I started I dined with the

Elgars at 58 New Cavendish Street, the flat they took from Mrs. Strong. I had a delightful evening, hearing all the news and also hearing a good deal of the E flat Symphony which was to be produced in the following year. I remember that I had various passages from the second movement singing in my head for days after.

I had a wonderful time in Florence, but it ended tragically. At breakfast, in my hotel, on May 8th, the nice elderly waiter who had taken charge of me and my meals all the while I had been there made his way over to my table obviously much concerned about something. 'Signorina,' he said, in a very low voice, 'il vostro Re è morto!' It made one feel as though one was at the Antipodes—I don't quite know why. The few other English people and I looked our grief and concern at one another and waited for further news. Next day I left for England and found myself a conspicuous object, in colours, when I landed; but I arrived home that evening decently clad.

Carice Elgar came to stay with us at Wolverhampton in July for our great annual Floral Fête. I think she enjoyed the flowers, the bands, and the fireworks as much as any of us.

In August that year (1910) we all went away on our usual summer holiday and Saturday morning, September 3rd, found me on my way to stay with Miss Danks at Gloucester for the Festival. I had heard from the Lady that they were taking a house on College Green, known as the Cookery School, for the week, and I was asked to bring Amy Danks to tea with them there on that Saturday. We got there early and I heard that several people were expected to tea besides the house-party, so there were lots of things that I could do to help the Lady.

Unusual noises were coming from somewhere upstairs and the Lady told me that Herr Kreisler and E. E. were going through the Violin Concerto behind locked doors! Having done all I could for the moment downstairs I went to look for Amy.

'Look here, I'm not going to miss all this. What about you?'

So we both slipped away upstairs and sat on the top step outside the door. It *was* interesting! Kreisler was trying bit after bit—not playing it properly, of course—but he was getting the composer's meaning and ideas. They did not speak one another's language very well and it was difficult at times. Kreisler became worried and anxious now and again and then at last he understood and raced off with it joyously. Loud applause from the piano. At last we tore ourselves away. Tea was coming in and the Lady might want me. There were a good many people there and we sat down to a long table.

'Will you sit at the end, dear Dora, and then when H. E. and Herr Kreisler come down perhaps you could stay and look after them if we've all done?'

That quite fitted in with my ideas, but we were hardly more than half-way through tea before the door opened and they came in. E. E. was in high spirits and demanded much tea, and I was introduced to Herr Kreisler and waited on them both. I do not know what the latter thought of it, or how much he understood of it, but he smiled when we laughed and I laughed so much I could hardly finish my tea.

'Did you see about the farewell to the missionaries, in the local paper, Dorabella?'

'No,' I said, putting down my cup for safety's sake. 'What happened?'

'Well, the paper said a party of them were being seen off at Foregate Street station and a large crow on the platform sang a hymn.'

That seemed to please him immensely.

Tea was finished at last and soon afterwards Amy and I left.

'Come to-morrow evening at about 9 o'clock, dear Dora, will you? and bring Miss Danks.' Then she added mysteriously: 'There's going to be something *quite interesting*!' But no more would she say and we speculated all the way home as to what it might be.

The opening service of the Festival was on Sunday afternoon and was hugely attended as it always is. Professor Sanford Terry, whom I had met at tea at the Elgars' the previous day, was one of the stewards.

The evening came at last.

'Let's be in good time,' I said. 'They won't mind, and you never know!'

But, early as we were, we heard a buzz of voices as we reached the door and the hall seemed to be nearly full of people already—mostly men, I noticed.

What *was* going to happen?

The piano that had been upstairs on the Saturday was now in the hall near a window, and a light was cleverly arranged near it; there was a music-stand by the piano and I saw Mr. W. H. Reed.

'It's the Violin Concerto!' I said to Amy Danks as we wormed our way to where the Lady was dispensing coffee.

'Dear Dora,' she said, 'you and Miss Danks must please pack yourselves away in a very small space,

85

there are many more coming than I expected and I'm *very* doubtful about the chairs!'

So we wedged ourselves into one of the two window-seats and were pretty close to the piano.

'My dear, *do* look at the pictures!'

Amy Danks, being herself an artist, had noticed before I had that all the pictures were turned round facing the wall. Some of them were draped with material and some were not.

'Isn't it too comic?' I said. 'I've known them do that elsewhere. I always want to go and peep behind to find out what they are.'

People were beginning to settle themselves now. I saw Professor Terry, Mr. Schuster, Dr. Brewer, Mr. Ivor Atkins, and Mr. Lee Williams among those present. It was a very warm evening; every door and window was open. People sat about all over the place, on the arms of chairs, up the stairs, and on the floor. 'No one minds if I play in my shirt-sleeves, I suppose,' said E. E., taking off his coat. 'You know I can't play this stuff.'

Then, to Mr. Atkins: 'You come and play the treble and I'll play the bass.'

Just before they began E. E. said in a low voice to Mr. Reed: 'You won't leave me alone in the tuttis, will you?'

I was half afraid that E. E. might indulge in his curious habit of 'singing' while he was playing. It was an odd noise: it seemed to be a kind of filling in of parts that he had not fingers enough to play. It was really more like grunting than singing. He actually did do it at the start, but whether it was that one became so absorbed, or whether he stopped doing it as anxiety

86

lessened I do not know. Nothing, however, spoilt the beauty of the performance. Mr. Reed evidently knew the Concerto inside out and played it splendidly. It really was glorious! And there were we among this select and privileged audience hearing it for the first time.

On the way back Amy Danks and I discussed ways and means for being together at the production in London in November.

The next day was filled with rehearsals in the Cathedral and I first met Mrs. Worthington, one of the many friends that the Elgars had made in the States, and I sat next her during the whole of the morning. Unfortunately none of E. E.'s music was rehearsed. I did so want to find out how much she knew of it and what her feelings about it were; but we had no opportunity of talking and, so far as I can remember, though I saw her every day during the Festival and we nodded and smiled to one another, I hardly spoke to her again.

On Friday morning it was *Messiah*. Professor Terry promised to take me up into the Triforium of the Choir for it—the Elgars usually heard it from up there—and as soon as the doors were shut and his duties as steward were over, I followed him up. At the top of the steps there was a flat space, rather gloomy and dark, and there was His Excellency, lying full length on three chairs, his head on a large red cushion, with arms folded over his chest and eyes shut. He heard our steps, and when he saw me he made an awful face and pointed with his thumb to the other side of the Triforium and shut his eyes again. Professor Terry and I went round to the north side where we found the Lady and Mrs. Worthington already established. We heard most beautifully, everything, words

87

and all (though knowing it almost by heart helps a good deal), but it must be remembered that all the singers had their backs to us—another testimonial, if one were needed, to the extraordinary merits of Gloucester Cathedral acoustically. It came through to us better than I could have imagined possible. And what a blessing it was to see no audience and no soloists and no mannerisms! One just heard the music without any hindrances. No wonder that E. E. chose that part of the Cathedral.

On November 10th, 1910, Amy Danks and I went together, as we had planned, to the Queen's Hall to hear the production of the Violin Concerto. The place was simply packed. Kreisler came on looking as white as a sheet—even for a player of his great experience it must have been a nervous moment—but he played superbly. E. E. was also, obviously, very much strung up; but all went well and the ovation at the end was tremendous. Kreisler and E. E. shook hands for quite a long while and they returned to bow their acknowledgements I don't know how often. Finally they came in arm-in-arm.

I do not seem to have heard anything of the Elgars all that winter—not even a Christmas card—but on March 27th, 1911, I had a card from him posted at Queenstown with a picture of a Cunard liner and the one word 'Goodbye'. He was off again to the States; this time, alone. I do not know how long he stayed there, but he was back in England for the London Musical Festival which took place at the end of May.

Sir Henry J. Wood conducted the Violin Concerto on the 23rd with Kreisler as soloist, and the Second

Symphony was produced on the 24th, conducted by the composer. That was another great success and E. E. got a fine ovation.

I wrote, as usual, for his birthday on June 2nd and received the following reply.

75 Gloucester Place
Portman Square. W.

My dear Child ('m, 'm!)   June 7, 1911

We are just back from the country where we successfully avoided

Music
Church
Noise

Heat & other disagreeables & got stung many times instead.

Thank you for your infantile prattle which was most inopportune—why remind me of my birthday?

(Mistaken wretch!)

This lovely phrase is what Hercules says in Handel's work to 'Pleasure' who invites him to the Dance, etc.

I like it: 'Mistaken wretch'—yes! its good and not too poetic.

Mistaken wretch!

It is hot: butter melts in the shade, also ice.

When are you coming? we are here for some time longer.

My love to all: but you should not remind me of my birthday: respeck the aged.

Mistaken wretch!

Yours disjointedly

The fifth letter: unless you count backwards.

P.S. The sanity of the writer (not of the writee) can be guaranteed for a small fee. If the receiver doubts the accuracy of the mess (!) age it can be repeated at half rates.

Among the Honours conferred at the Coronation of King George V (June 22nd, 1911) appeared

SIR EDWARD ELGAR, *Order of Merit.*

I HAD been a good deal laughed at at home for my championship of Elgar. I am afraid that they accused me of an admiration for his music to the exclusion of all other composers. This was hardly fair and the accusation was quite unjustified. Anyhow, E. E. was always alluded to as 'The Only Composer'! It was not until the Coronation Honours were published in June, 1911, that this title was abandoned for another: 'The O.M.' now took its place.

The Elgars left Hereford early in the New Year and went to live at Hampstead. I had a card from Professor Sanford Terry dated January 22nd, 1912, which ended:

> The E's are settling into 42. Netherhall Gardens. I lit the first fire in the Dining Room 10 days ago! He is very happy and working at the Masque.[1] C. S. T.

Severn House (as they called their new home) had a very large and beautifully panelled studio which made a magnificent music-room. When I first saw it there were no less than three pianos, a grand and two uprights, and there was plenty of room for them as well as for most of his other study furniture. Off this large room opened a small one, partly lined with bookshelves, which he used as a study.

'You *are* in clover here,' I said, 'and fancy having a study as well!'

'I don't know about the clover—I've left that behind at Hereford—but Hereford is too far away from London; that's the trouble. Look here, do you

---

[1] *The Crown of India.*

Histed

SIR EDWARD ELGAR: O.M.

June 1911

see that I've got room for a billiard-table? Perhaps you'll see it the next time you come.'

I heard some of the Masque that day and also some of *The Music Makers*. After playing the passage which ends 'The singer who sings no more', he said:

'How do you like that?'

But I could not answer. Thinking of Nimrod I turned away and said presently:

'That's going to be terribly trying to listen to. Bringing in "Novissima hora est" there is simply wonderful.'

I did not see them again till the Birmingham Festival the following October. On the Tuesday evening we had the production of *The Music Makers* with Muriel Foster as soloist and I have no words to describe how beautifully she sang it. Dear 'Small German'! How he would have loved it!

There was a very fine performance of *The Apostles* on the Friday evening and we saw the Lady for a few minutes afterwards. Sir Edward conducted both *Apostles* and *Music Makers*, so there was no chance of seeing him—except his back!

I lunched with them at Severn House on April 12th, 1913, and he played me a good deal of *Falstaff*.

I did not see them again till we met at the Gloucester Festival. There was a fine performance of *Gerontius* on the Tuesday and the Second Symphony was on the Thursday morning.

I heard *Gerontius* for the sixteenth time at Birmingham, in October, and heard *Falstaff*, the Variations, and the Second Symphony at the Queen's Hall, conducted by Landon Ronald, in November.

In the spring of 1914 I paid my last visit to the

Elgars. I had married in the previous January, and I took my husband to see them and make their acquaintance. I kept in touch with them by being, still, Keeper of the Archives; but here my memories end.

CONCLUSION

IN this book I have tried to show what Edward Elgar was like before he rose to fame and in the early years of his success. The incidents I have described and the stories I have told are all true: I have nowhere given rein to imagination.

Various competent writers have dealt with the technical side of his art and I have left the subject of his music, as such, severely alone. But the number of those who knew him forty years ago is becoming very small indeed and that is my reason for putting together these recollections of the greatest composer this country has yet produced.

Many people seem to think that a great creative artist must be more or less eccentric and a law unto himself. To them probably the most remarkable thing about Elgar, apart from his musical ability, is that he was sane and normal. He liked and enjoyed ordinary things—fun and nonsense, games and sports, birds and beasts—and was temperate and controlled. He loved his wife and he loved his home. I have always thought that his sanity is reflected in his music which, however original, is never freakish and never morbid.

Elgar's attitude towards music was curiously unprofessional. He hated teaching music and, in general, he disliked talking about it. He always pretended that he knew nothing about it, which was often funny and sometimes a little tiresome.

When I was turning over for him I could sometimes get answers to questions, or little comments and explanations, and occasionally, when we were out together he would begin singing a bit out of a Beethoven Sonata or Symphony (if I could join in we used to make quite a noise), and then he would discuss the music and give me his views on it.

As may be imagined, when I arrived on a visit my greatest wish was to hear new music; but sometimes he would not touch the subject of music at all and, to gain my selfish ends, I have even resorted to guile and subtlety. I have gone to the length of singing a tune incorrectly on purpose.

'That's wrong. Don't you know it goes like this?'

Then of course he would play it and one thing led to another. I have heard it said that he took no interest in any music but his own. This is not the case. I have heard him play *Parsifal* and *Die Meistersinger* and many passages from Mozart, Beethoven, and Brahms. I have spoken of his playing Bach. He used to say that you should begin the day by playing a Bach Fugue. I do not think he actually did it himself—perhaps it was an ideal to be aimed at. He and Mr. Atkins[1] brought out an edition of the *St. Matthew Passion* (1911). He introduced me to *Phoebus and Pan* and played most of it to me at various times. He greatly admired the orchestration of Richard Strauss and Berlioz. In the region of lighter music he had a distinct weakness for the Gilbert and Sullivan operas.

He himself had a flair for this kind of music. I remember hearing the delightful merry tunes he had written in early days for a children's operetta.

'Those *are* capital tunes,' I said; 'almost as good as Sullivan!'

'*Almost* as good? Listen to this . . . and this . . .',

[1] Now Sir Ivor Atkins.

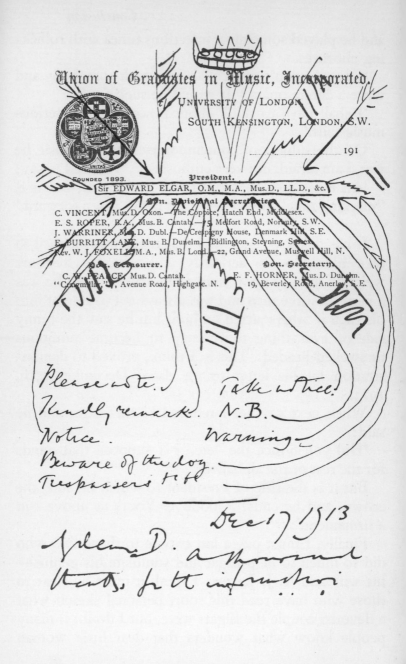

Union of Graduates in Music, Incorporated.

UNIVERSITY OF LONDON
SOUTH KENSINGTON, LONDON, S.W.

191

FOUNDED 1893.   **President.**

Sir EDWARD ELGAR, O.M., M.A., Mus.D., LL.D., &c.

Hon. Divisional Secretaries.

C. VINCENT, Mus.D. Oxon.—The Coppice, Hatch End, Middlesex.
E. S. ROPER, B.A., Mus.B. Cantab.—5 Melfort Road, Norbury, S.W.
J. WARRINER, Mus.D. Dubl.—De Crespigny House, Denmark Hill, S.E.
F. BURRITT LANE, Mus. B. Dunelm.—Bidlington, Steyning, Sussex.
Rev. W. J. FOXELL, M.A., Mus.B. Lond.—22, Grand Avenue, Muswell Hill, N.

Hon. Treasurer.   **Hon. Secretary.**

C. W. PEARCE, Mus.D. Cantab.   E. F. HORNER, Mus.D. Dunelm.
"Cragmullan," 4, Avenue Road, Highgate. N.   19, Beverley Road, Anerley, S.E.

Please note.   *Take notice!*
Kindly remark.   *N.B.*
Notice.   *Warning*
Beware of the dog.
Trespassers &c &c

Dec 17 1513

*[signature] D. a thousand
thanks for the information*

and he played some most infectious tunes with rollicking choruses.

'Oh, *why* don't you collaborate with somebody and write a comic opera? It would be such fun!'

'I shall have to think about it some day if serious music fails.'

On the subject of contemporary English music he was, I am afraid, not very enthusiastic. He used to say:

'All these men turn out fairly good stuff, but it is "marking time" all the while and never a step forward.'

It has, I know, been said that Elgar was inclined to take himself very seriously and that his honours weighed heavily upon him. The truth is that he was a very sensitive man and was always apt to retreat into his shell if others jarred on him; but he saw the funny side of everything too clearly to become pompous or swelled-headed. This is, I think, proved to demonstration by his letter to me dated December 17th, 1913.

When next we met I referred to this letter and he said:

'Did you notice the "etc."? I suppose that stands for the rest of the alphabet!'

But it is the title of President to which he adds the crown, and he ends: 'Goodbye. Yours as above—in a firmament.'

Finally, I must pay a last tribute to those two who did so much to help Elgar and stimulate his genius—his wife and A. J. Jaeger. I think it must be clear to those who have read this short personal sketch what a devoted couple the Elgars were, but I doubt if many people know what wonders that dear little woman wrought. Her efforts on his behalf were untiring. With single-minded devotion she spent herself unceasingly to help and encourage him. She schemed and planned, suggested and persuaded, while aiding and abetting him in all that he did. She contrived that he should meet the right people, saved him from troublesome interviews, and always did what she could to keep worries from him. She spent hours preparing orchestral score-paper and ruling bar-lines and, in addition, she did all the general secretarial work.

Often she had to be very patient. There were days when he felt disinclined for work and other times when work took possession of him and he could hardly be persuaded to stop for food or even for sleep.

In all the years I knew them I never heard anything like a cross word.

Elgar's dependence on her was such that it is small wonder to me that, after her death, he had little heart for composition.

She was indeed an ideal wife for a genius!

Mr. Jaeger was, so far as I know, the only musician with whom Elgar discussed his work in technical detail. His criticisms and advice always received the composer's careful consideration even if the suggestions were not always adopted. It was Mr. Jaeger who suggested the lengthening of the Finale of the Variations which led to the addition of another hundred bars. I was at Malvern when the proof of the new ending arrived and E. E. played it to me and roared with laughter, thoroughly enjoying what he had written.

'The old Moss was right,' he said.

Nimrod's own view is expressed in a letter to me
dated April 10th, 1907:

I have worked terribly hard for E. E. and ruined my health
over it very likely. . . .

I have never loved & admired a man more, made myself
more a slave for any man out of sheer enthusiasm.

APPENDIX

It is well known that Elgar was always interested in puzzles, ciphers, cryptograms, and the like. The cipher here reproduced—the third letter I had from him, if indeed it is one—came to me enclosed in a letter from the Lady to my mother. On the back of it is written, 'Miss Penny'. It followed upon their visit to us at Wolverhampton in July 1897 (see p. 9).

I have never had the slightest idea what message it conveys; he never explained it and all attempts to solve it have failed. Should any reader of this book succeed in arriving at a solution it would interest me very much to hear of it.

PRINTED IN
GREAT BRITAIN
AT THE
UNIVERSITY PRESS
OXFORD
BY
JOHN JOHNSON
PRINTER
TO THE
UNIVERSITY